TRADITIONAL BOATBUILDING MADE EASY

Building Catherine

a 14 foot pulling boat in the whitehall tradition

TRADITIONAL BOATBUILDING MADE EASY

Building Catherine

a 14 foot pulling boat in the whitehall tradition

A WoodenBoat Book
by Richard Kolin

Book design by Lindy Gifford and Tim Seymour

Cover design by Lindy Gifford

Jane Crosen, editor

Printed in the United States of America

Cover photographs by Marty Loken

Photographs on pages 3, 4, and 5 are from the
collection of the San Francisco Maritime
National Historical Park.

A WoodenBoat Book
ISBN 0-937822-62-0
www.woodenboat.com

Acknowledgements

I am having a lot of fun with the *Traditional Boatbuilding Made Easy* series; it gives me the chance to work with friends new and old. By building traditional wooden boats, I meet some wonderful people while I am helping them, they are helping me, or we are just talking about my favorite subject, wooden small craft. Every now and then I have to stop and say thank you to some of them.

My wife Catherine gets the most thanks. When she married me she didn't have a clue what she was getting into, and she has held up in fine style. Charlie Allen of Santa Cruz, California, is a consummate boatbuilder who encouraged me in the early days when I needed it most. Bob and Erica Picket of Flounder Bay Boat Lumber in Anacortes, Washington, have proved what perseverance in the face of impossible odds can do by starting a specialty lumber business and keeping it alive. They have been the starting point of many a fledgling boatbuilder. Peter Spectre, whom I first met some 25 years ago, was the driving force behind getting this series into print. Dick Wagner is the founder of The Center for Wooden Boats in Seattle and a friend for the past 30 years. Dick is an institution in his own right and has been one of the guiding lights of the revival of interest in building wooden small craft. The Center for Wooden Boats is the realization of my mentor, John Gardner's, vision. Those of us who support it and nurture it are aware of our responsibility to keep the dream alive. Discovering the history of the Whitehall boat can be difficult, and much remains to be researched. In particular we need to know more of the small-craft boatbuilding scene in New York in the period of 1800 to 1850 and the influence of English boatbuilders. To my knowledge, the most complete historical essay on the Whitehall boat, its origins, and its construction are Chapters 21 and 22 in John Gardner's book *Building Classic Small Craft*. My small effort was greatly enhanced by research support from the Smithsonian Institution in Washington, D.C., the J. Porter Shaw Library of the National Maritime Museum in San Francisco, The California Historical Society, the research staff at WoodenBoat, and of course the writings of John Gardner, W. P. Stephens, Capt. Charlton L. Smith, and Howard I. Chapelle.

And thanks to all of you out there who are building wooden boats and using them. You are members of a small but ever-growing crew of people who are helping to preserve an important link with the past by adapting old skills and technologies to today's world.

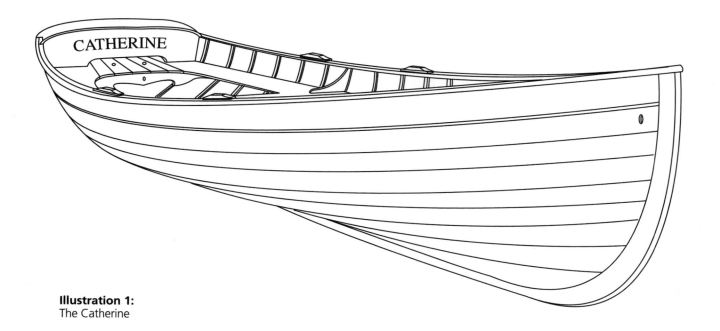

Illustration 1:
The Catherine

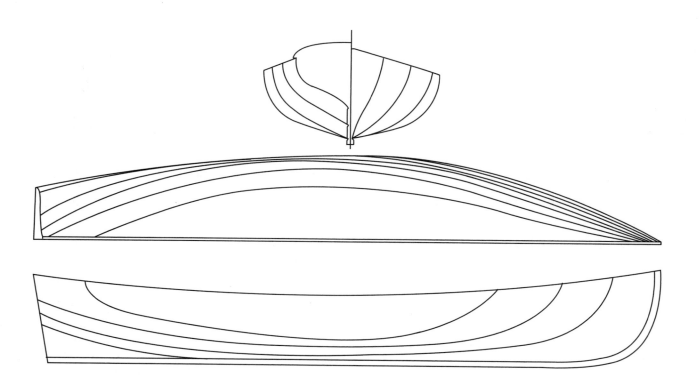

Illustration 2:
The lines

Introduction

No other boat seems to grab the attention more than a well-turned-out Whitehall. Its lean, clean lines and shapely hull cleave the water with hardly a wake. It is the epitome of Victorian grace whether propelled by oars or by sail.

When the publishers at WoodenBoat Books suggested that I make the Whitehall boat the second book in our Traditional Boatbuilding Made Easy series, there was no hesitation. Anyone interested in building traditional small boats should have more than a passing knowledge of this wonderful craft.

I first come upon the idea for this series after I spent my early years as a boatbuilder desperately trying to glean enough information, bit by bit from many different books, to build my first boat. Each of these books was trying to cover the whole field of wooden boat building in a few hundred pages. When I tried to learn in detail how to build one boat, I found many questions unanswered or vague. I finally built up enough courage to start anyway and figured it out as I went. After several boats, I began to get the hang of it, but I was left with the feeling that I had learned the hard way. Many years later, after 30 years of building boats, working in a variety of boatyards, and finally teaching boatbuilding, I decided what was needed was a series of books that would focus on building one boat, using one type of construction; this would keep the learning process as simple as possible. The result was *Traditional Boatbuilding Made Easy: Heidi, a 12-foot skiff for oar and sail.* The response of first-time boatbuilders has been overwhelming. The concept works, and so I went to work on this, the second book in the series.

In the first book I realized that I need to teach two construction variations, the traditional method and modifications to the traditional method brought about by new adhesives and the popularity of trailering small craft. I will describe the pros and cons of both, and the builder can decide which he or she prefers.

The 12-foot skiff is still the best boat for the beginning boatbuilder who has limited experience with hand tools. This second book takes off where the first book ends and gives the intermediate builder new challenges. Does this mean that if you have not built a boat before you shouldn't build this boat? No, but it does mean that you should give the project careful study before you begin, and you must understand the commitment it requires in time, space, money, and mental distraction. I would recommend that a newcomer take one of the boatbuilding classes offered around the country by a variety of maritime museums (such as Mystic Seaport in Connecticut) and boat schools (such as The Center for Wooden Boats in Seattle, and Woodenboat School in Brooklin, Maine). This is a good time to begin to be a wooden boat builder, with so many good sources of information, materials, and experience available.

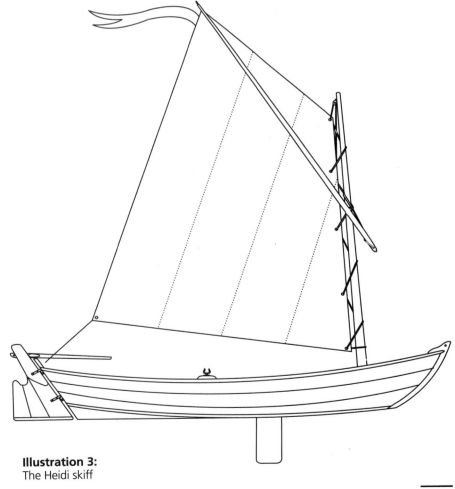

Illustration 3:
The Heidi skiff

I

In the Beginning

Learning to build wooden boats, then and now

Some years ago I was doing field research on a unique boat that evolved at Willippa Bay, just north of the mouth of the Columbia River in Washington state. I had the privilege of meeting Marion Lauderbeck, whose father Dan was a legendary boatbuilder in the area. Marion learned his trade from his father, and his son was learning from him. In times past, boatbuilders learned on the job from the master and journeyman craftsmen at the local shop or yard. The closely guarded secret techniques were the only job security boatbuilders had, and the young apprentices had to be watchful to learn what they needed know to achieve journeyman status. The lucky ones had fathers who would spend the time to pass on the secrets of the trade. Yet Marion, 92 years old and just retired when I met with him, noted that he didn't know as much as his father and his son would never know as much as he did. This is a direct result of the demise of wooden boat building in the 20th century.

So where does that leave the rest of us? I have seen the wooden boat building yards disappear one after the other. At one time it appeared that the skills of wooden boat building would disappear altogether. The reason this did not come to pass was largely the work of Howard Chapelle and John Gardner and a host of maritime museums (Mystic Seaport comes to mind), apprenticeship programs, local community colleges and trade schools, WoodenBoat, International Marine Publishing, and small-craft builders who are willing, for little compensation, to write down their hard-won lessons. The new boatbuilder is an amateur who is willing to spend a few dollars and much spare time learning what can be learned from books and classes, and building some very beautiful and useful boats.

The origins and myths of the Whitehall boat

The origins of the Whitehall boat are misty at best. W. P. Stephens, the noted small-craft historian, thought the type originated at Whitehall Street in New York City in the 1820s.[1] Other reports say the boat originated in Whitehall, England. Wherever it originated, by the time the clipper ships reached prominence, the Whitehall boat was frequently mentioned in literature describing waterfront activities.[4] It continued as a dominant feature of waterfront commerce until the small, inexpensive gasoline engine emerged in the early 20th century. In the late 19th century, in Boston, Capt. Charlton Smith counted 75 working Whitehalls at "The Hub" and another 19 in the "Cow Pen."[2] During the same period, Tom Crowley, a San Francisco Whitehall boatman, reported 80 to 100 working Whitehalls in San Francisco.[3]

The Whitehall boat performed the function of a water taxi. It ferried captains, businessmen, newspaper reporters, government functionaries, and assorted waterfront characters to and from ships arriving at the major harbors of the United States. Ed McCarthy, who was a San Francisco Whitehall boatman at the end of the Whitehall period, claimed: "When word came in from the lookouts that a ship was on the way in, the boatmen would all pile into their boats and race out to her. In each boat would usually be a chronometer man, a butcher, a grocer, a ship stores man. The first boatload would get all of her business while she was in port."[9]

The working Whitehall boats were generally 17 to 20 feet in length, 4 feet 6 to 8 inches in beam, about 20 inches deep, and weighed over 250 pounds. The type spread rapidly and is best known in relation to New York, Boston, and later San Francisco,[4] although it was used extensively in most harbors. In time, the Whitehall became the dominant influence on the design and construction of small yacht tenders and rowing boats through most of the 19th and early 20th centuries.[7]

Tom Crowley was still around when I talked to him in the early 1970s. I wish I could have asked more questions. Fortunately, he left a record of his experiences as a Whitehall boatman in San Francisco.[3] He learned about the San Francisco waterfront from his stepfather, who had made a name for himself as a Whitehall boatman and earned the nickname "Hook-on Crowley." The stories of Tom and his father are typical of the lives of the Whitehall boatmen and how they plied their trade. Tom started his career as a boat boy in 1890 when he was 14, and launched his own Whitehall service the following year.

The boatman usually had aboard another man representing some shoreside business competing for the trade of the incoming sailing ships. Lookouts on the coast would spot the incoming ships and telegraph the marine exchange on the waterfront. The marine exchange was operated by the merchants and was the information center for the marine-related businesses. When competition was great, the boats went far out into the open ocean and waited for the ships to arrive. According to Tom, there could be as many as 18 to 20 ships a day arriving in San Francisco. The San Francisco boatman carried no food and water aboard as a matter of pride and relied on passing ships for sustenance. A set of oilskins and a bailer were his only protection from the elements. Each boat carried a hook shaped like a shepherd's crook with 30 fathoms of line. The boatman would row out to a passing steam schooner or tug and hook on to the chains (attached to the hull, that led to the shrouds supporting the mast), let out enough line to clear the wake, and ride out past the harbor entrance. The competition was tough, and only the strong survived.

The Whitehall boatman's passenger many times was a boardinghouse runner. The runner's job was to contract with the captain of the incoming ship to provide a new crew. At the same time he would try to talk the crew on board into staying at his boardinghouse. He would regale them with stories of wild women and good liquor, sometimes even persuading crew members to jump ship on the spot. When the sailor's money was gone, the runner promised to get him a good ship. Young Tom Crowley stayed in the boat when he rowed out a runner, as he couldn't stand to hear the lies. It was a predatory system, and the sailors were the prey. It was these boardinghouses that invented the term "shanghaiing." This was the practice of bartenders drugging an unsuspecting customer, a sailor or landsman who, much to his surprise, would waken on a ship bound for Shanghai. There are stories of dead men being dumped on the deck of a ship hidden among the drunken sailors.[8] The harsh life of the ordinary seaman was the scandal of the period and led to many reforms by the dawning of the new century.

The runner existed due to a tradition of the ship captains that they would pay off the crew upon docking. Longshoremen unloaded the cargo, so deckhands were not needed. After loading a new cargo, the captain would need a new crew quickly. The boardinghouse runner provided this service. In a large sailing ship, that could be as many as 22 crewmen.[8]

On December 9, 1824, the 27-foot racing gig *American Star* beat the British gig *Hussar* in front of a crowd of 50,000 spectators in New York Harbor. The population of New York City at that time was under 150,000, so that was quite a turnout. In newspapers of the time, the American rowers were called "Whitehallers," which would indicate that the word Whitehall and rowing were already interlocked. Using the hardy professional waterfront oarsman as a racing crew made sense. *American Star* was presented to General Lafayette upon his visit to the United States in 1824–25 and still exists under the care of his descendants at his ancestral chateau. The story of *American Star* and the replica that was built at Mystic Seaport is told in John Gardner's book, *Wooden Boats to Build and Use*.[5]

Thomas Crowley bought his first Whitehall for $80. He eventually bought three more Whitehall boats and hired his two stepbrothers, David and John, and a boatman called Dutch Albert. Tom described the San Francisco Whitehall boat as being 18 feet long and 4 feet 8 inches in the beam. In 1904, he built his first gasoline-powered launch. That was the end of the Whitehall boats; the power launch could service many ships at the same time, the Whitehall only one. This humble beginning developed into a multinational corporation called Crowley Maritime Corporation.

No boats of the working Whitehall period exist. Most of our small working craft were discarded and forgotten when the boats were no longer needed. The surviving examples of the Whitehall type are smaller or of lighter construction, indicating that they were used as pleasure boats. Fortunately, the Whitehall was an inspiration to many builders who built boats that were used for pleasure, thus preserving their construction and design details.[6] Maritime historians have recorded the lines and construction details of many of these boats and have made them available for study. Mystic Seaport Museum is a leader in this field and has developed plans from its small-craft collection that are available to the public at a modest price (see "Sources," at the end of Chapter II). Many other maritime museums have followed Mystic Seaport's lead. The Smithsonian Institution also has available a catalog of its collection of plans which includes four Whitehall boats (see *Ship Plan List* in the reference list following this section).

The design elements of the Whitehall boat—the long, narrow, double-ended waterline, plumb stem, moderate deadrise (angle of the bottom to the keel), and high, tucked transom—are common to many of the working boats used in the 19th century and have roots deep into American and European nautical history. The combination of these elements into a fast, yet hardy workboat, designed for a crew of one or two and one or two passengers, captured the interest of waterfront boatmen and influenced generations of boatbuilders to build Whitehall boats following the same general dimensions and construction details. The annual workboat races, usually held on the Fourth of July, and the demands of rowing clubs further led to the refinement and standardization of the design. The boats were usually built locally, but some builders shipped their boats to other harbors. Tom Crowley, several times the winner of the Fourth of July Whitehall boat races (as was his stepfather before him), remembered that local San Francisco builders had competition from a builder named Everson whose boats were built at Elizabeth, New Jersey.[3] Apparently his boats could be built and shipped across the country at a competitive price.

In the 19th century, lapstrake was the popular construction form for racing and pleasure craft, and carvel (smooth skin) for working Whitehall boats. A skilled craftsman could plank a boat in the carvel manner more quickly, and many oarsmen felt that the smooth skin of the carvel-planked boat moved through open waters better than the ultralight lapstrake boats. By the latter half of the 19th century, the elements of construction of the working Whitehall had been standardized (see Figure 1). The boats were carvel-planked of ½-inch cedar with a ⅝-inch oak sheerstrake lapped over the next plank, called the binder. Frames sided ¾ inch (thickness) were bent in pairs over molds with a greater curve than

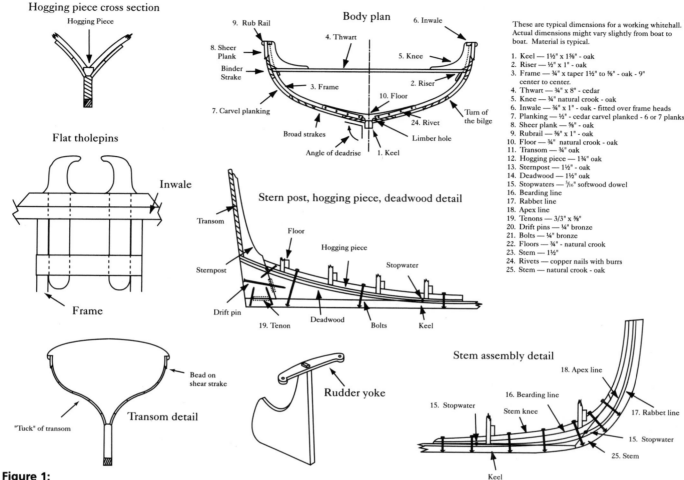

Hogging piece cross section

Hogging Piece

Flat tholepins

Inwale

Frame

Bead on
shear strake

"Tuck" of transom

Transom detail

Rudder yoke

Body plan

9. Rub Rail

4. Thwart

6. Inwale

8. Sheer
Plank

5. Knee

Binder
Strake

2. Riser

3. Frame

7. Carvel planking

10. Floor

Broad strakes

24. Rivet

Turn of
the bilge

Angle of deadrise

Limber hole

1. Keel

Stern post, hogging piece, deadwood detail

Transom

Floor

Sternpost

Hogging piece

Stopwater

Drift pin

19. Tenon

Deadwood

Bolts

Keel

Stem assembly detail

18. Apex line

16. Bearing line

15. Stopwater

Stem knee

17. Rabbet line

15. Stopwater

25. Stem

Keel

These are typical dimensions for a working whitehall.
Actual dimensions might vary slightly from boat to
boat. Material is typical.

1. Keel — 1½" x 1⅝" - oak
2. Riser — ½" x 1" - oak
3. Frame — ¾" x taper 1½" to ⅝" - oak - 9"
   center to center.
4. Thwart — ¾" x 8" - cedar
5. Knee — ¾" natural crook - oak
6. Inwale — ¾" x 1" - oak - fitted over frame heads
7. Planking — ½" - cedar carvel planked - 6 or 7 planks
8. Sheer plank — ⅝" - oak
9. Rubrail — ⅝" x 1" - oak
10. Floor — ¾" natural crook - oak
11. Transom — ¾" oak
12. Hogging piece — 1¾" oak
13. Sternpost — 1½" - oak
14. Deadwood — 1½" oak
15. Stopwaters — 5/16" softwood dowel
16. Bearding line
17. Rabbet line
18. Apex line
19. Tenons — 3/3" x ⅝"
20. Drift pins — ¼" bronze
21. Bolts — ¼" bronze
22. Floors — ¾" - natural crook
23. Stem — 1½"
24. Rivets — copper nails with burrs
25. Stem — natural crook - oak

Figure 1:
Construction details of the working whitehall boat

the actual shape of the boat. When they were needed, they were tapered, usually from 1 to 1⅜ inches at the butt to ½ to ¾ inch at the sheer, then beveled on their outer face (and sometimes the inner as well). Ribbands (wooden stringers) were bent around molds set up on a jig or nailed to the floor. The pre-bent frames were set up in position inside the ribbands and pulled into the shape of the boat. A bent frame cannot be bent further after steaming, but can be relaxed. The frames were set up and riveted to floor timbers running across the keel. There was no keel batten. A piece of wood called a hogging piece was attached to the top of the deadwood to give the planks there more backing. At the sheer, a one-piece gunwale (inwale) was fitted over the frame heads and inside the sheerstrake. The boats were rowed with flat tholepins mortised into the gunwale. This construction varied slightly from location to location. A centerboard was often fitted, and a spritsail with a jib was the usual sailing rig. The boat was steered with a yoke and lines.

Today there is a more generic description of the Whitehall boat, and it is more than likely to be built of lapstrake construction. While it retains the design elements of the working Whitehall, the construction is totally different. The length can be anywhere from 12 to 20 feet, and beam can be either side of 4 feet. It is generally lighter, of less beam, and not as deep as the working Whitehall, as dictated by its use as a pleasure boat.

Bibliography and recommended reading

1. Stephens, W. P., unpublished article "Old-Time Boat Building in New York," April 6, 1935. Manuscript returned to him March 20, 1940. Smithsonian, National Museum of American History, Washington, DC 20560-MRC628. W. P. Stephens (1854–1946) was the first historian to try to capture the history and construction of the working Whitehall boat and his writings are an important resource to all the historians who followed.

2. Smith, Capt. Charlton L., "The Whitehall Boat," *The Rudder*, August 1943. Capt. Smith was a correspondent and collaborator of W. P. Stephens who was able to fill in Stephens's research with important details of Whitehall boat construction methods and details. This article was the last published before his death.

3. Kortum, Karl, *Thomas Crowley, Recollection of the San Francisco Waterfront*. An interview conducted by Karl Kortum and Willa Klug Baum, University of California, Bancroft Library, Berkeley, 1967. (From the San Francisco Maritime Museum J. Porter Shaw Library, Building E, Fort Mason Center, San Francisco, CA 94123). An oral history of a Whitehall boatman who built his small fleet of Whitehall boats into a major multinational corporation. All references to Tom Crowley come from this source.

4. Chapelle, Howard I., *American Small Sailing Craft, Their Design, Development and Construction*, W. W. Norton & Company, New York, 1951. This is the bible of small-craft builders, with its descriptions of many small boats that were too good to die out. It includes the basic Whitehall story, with plans and construction details of two Whitehall boats. Full-sized plans for these and all the other boats in this book are available from the Smithsonian Institution.

5. Gardner, John, *Wooden Boats to Build and Use*, Mystic Seaport Museum, Mystic, Connecticut, 1996. Includes the history of the racing gig *American Star*, the oldest American-built racing rowboat in existence.

6. Bray, Maynard, *Mystic Seaport Museum Watercraft*, Mystic Seaport Museum, Inc., Mystic, Connecticut, 1979. This is a catalog of the Mystic Seaport small-craft collection with photographs. It includes the Seaport's collection of Whitehall boats and their near kin, with some lines and construction details. Mystic has a program of documenting important craft in its collection, and plans are available from the Seaport.

7. Gardner, John, *Building Classic Small Craft*, International Marine Publishing Company, Camden, Maine, 1977. Chapter 21 is the definitive discussion of the origins of the Whitehall boat. Chapter 22 includes plans, construction details, and building instructions for a carvel-planked Whitehall boat of Gardner's own design in the spirit of the working Whitehall.

8. Morris, Paul C., *A Portrait of a Ship, The Benjamin F. Packard*, Lower Cape Publishing, Orleans, Massachusetts, 1987. The story of the life and death of a Maine-built Down Easter, and the end of the sailing era. It describes the economics and culture of a wooden sailing ship, and shows the Whitehall boat as a vital link between the landsmen and the ships in the maritime economy.

9. O'Brien, Robert, "Riptides: at the End of the Hyde Street Wharf," *San Francisco Chronicle*, November 13, 15, and 17, 1950. A three-part interview with Edward F. McCarthy, a Whitehall boatman in the last days of the Whitehall boat in San Francisco. (The California Historical Society, 2090 Jackson Street, San Francisco, CA 94109.)

10. *Ship Plan List*, National Museum of American History, Smithsonian Institution, Washington, D.C. Inquiries to: Ship Plans, Division of Transportation, NMAH – 5010/MRC 628, Smithsonian Institution, Washington, DC 20560. The catalog of plans and photographs of ships and boats in the Smithsonian collection, including all plans from the published works of Howard I. Chapelle, Harry V. Sucher, the Historic American Merchant Marine Survey, and Howard I. Chapelle's collection of yachts and small craft. Gives modelmakers, historians, and small-craft builders inexpensive access to a treasure trove of information.

Additional reading

Bridgewater, Alan and Gill, *Carving Figureheads & Other Nautical Designs*, Sterling Publishing Co., Inc., New York, 1995.

Culler, R. D., *Boats, Oars, and Rowing*, International Marine Publishing, Camden, Maine, 1978.

Culler, R. D., *Skiffs and Schooners*, International Marine Publishing, Camden, Maine, 1974.

Gardner, John, *Classic Small Craft You Can Build*, Mystic Seaport Museum, Mystic, Connecticut, 1993.

Hanna, Jay S., *The Shipcarver's Handbook*, WoodenBoat Books, Brooklin, Maine, 1988.

Kingshott, Jim, *Sharpening, The Complete Guide*, Guild of Master Craftsman Publications Ltd., 166 High Street, Lewes, East Sussex BN7 1XU, England, 1994.

Marino, Emiliano, *The Sailmaker's Apprentice, A Guide for the Self-Reliant Sailor*, International Marine, Camden, Maine, 1994.

Rössel, Greg, *Building Small Boats*, WoodenBoat Books, Brooklin, Maine, 1998.

Spectre, Peter, Series Editor, *Painting and Varnishing*, WoodenBoat Books, Brooklin, Maine, 1995.

Spectre, Peter, Series Editor, *Planking and Fastening*, WoodenBoat Books, Brooklin, Maine, 1996.

Spielman, Patrick, *Sharpening Basics*, Sterling Publishing Co., Inc., New York, 1991.

White, Paul, *Carving a Traditional Cape Cod Sign*, Shiffer Publishing Ltd., Atglen, Pennsylvania, 1994.

Lapstrake boatbuilding, then and now

Traditional lapstrake boatbuilding is the ultimate in lightweight plank-on-frame construction. The fore-and-aft laps add to structural strength and allow a reduction in plank and frame thickness while increasing the overall stiffness of the boat. The thin planking reduces the amount swelling and shrinking when in and out of the water, and favors boats that might not be kept in the water all season. The cost of this lighter weight is a building method that is more complicated than the carvel planking methods favored by the working watermen of the late 19th century.

Despite the added complexity, traditional lapstrake construction adheres to the same basic principle that guides all plank-on-frame boatbuilding: Tightly fitted joints, well fastened, when swelled by water, are watertight. This tight fit is ensured at the plank ends by the addition of cotton caulking forced into the plank seams at the stem and transom end by a caulking wheel (designed like a small pizza cutter). The caulking is made continuous by leaving a small tuft of cotton at the end of each strand which is worked into the beginning of the new strand. An oil-based seam compound is then inserted in the seam over the cotton.

The caulking cotton serves several purposes. The first is to wedge the seams tightly together. The second is to wick water from the below-the-waterline seams to those above, ensuring that all the seams in the boat remain tight. The third is to hold moisture in the seams as long as possible, allowing the boat to remain tight even when out of the water for short periods of time.

Bedding compounds, commonly used today under the planking at the stem, or in the laps of lapstrake planking, were not often used in the past. In the traditional carvel-planked construction method (Figure 1), cotton caulking and oil-based seam compound form a flexible sealant in the seam at the plank ends. This seam compound eventually loses its flexibility and has to be replaced periodically.

If the boat is left out of the water for a time, joints in the stem and deadwood assembly tend to open, allowing water to seep into the boat upon relaunching. To combat this, stopwaters, softwood dowels, are driven tightly into holes drilled in the stem and deadwood joints in the deepest part (the apex) of the rabbet, under the planking. Water seeping into the joint reaches the softwood stopwater, which swells faster than the hardwood around it, shutting off the water channel. The tightly fitted planks close off the ends of the stopwaters to aid in water retention. For this to work well, all wood-to-wood fits need to be tight and the boat has to be either in the water all the time, or out of the water for only a short period.

Throughout the history of wooden boats there have been attempts to develop design or construction modifications that reduce or eliminate leaks when the boats are subjected to prolonged periods out of the water. One of these was batten-seam planking, a carvel planking method (planks fitted edge-to-edge) in which the seams were backed up with battens, achieving the tight-lapped effect of lapstrake. This method was widely used in building the whaleboats of the 19th century. Batten-seam and lapstrake planking both worked on the principle that in the narrow cross-sections of the plank, swelling is reduced, increasing the likelihood that the plank would remain tight. J. Henry Rushton, a well-known builder of lightweight sport canoes at the turn of the 19th century, used various forms of lapped planking methods and attempted to seal the seams with thick varnish. This was a common practice in lightweight construction during this period. Many other builders of this period would use cotton soaked with thick varnish as a bedding compound at the stem and transom.

Modern adhesives have improved the possibility of watertight craft by providing gap-filling, waterproof capability. This has been at the expense of increased cost in material, along with increases in application and cleanup time. Adhesives such as the widely used polyurethane adhesive compounds are so strong that they make repairs such as plank or stem replacement extremely difficult. In effect, the builder is gluing the boat together with an elastic adhesive.

Ideally, our bedding compound should allow for the disassembly of the parts. Polyurethane adhesives won't allow this. In days past, polysulfides were used for bedding. They worked fairly well, but adhesion was not always the best. Polysulfides have been largely replaced by polyurethane bedding compounds. The most common are 3M 4200 and Sikaflex 341.

I have also had good results with various bathroom caulks. These are usually some form of acrylic latex commonly available at most hardware stores; some include silicone. All the caulks that I have used have been designated by the manufacturer as paintable and suitable for marine use. They seem to be perfect for the job. They can be cleaned up with water, can be cut with sharp tools, and allow for disassembly. Their drawback is that in the fine print the manufacturers say that they are not for below-waterline use. For this reason, I cannot recommend them. All I can say that I have not had any problems with them, but I have not used them in boats that have been subjected to prolonged immersion.

Some lapstrake builders reject the modern adhesives because of the problems with disassembly, and use more traditional oil-based bedding compounds at the stem and in the gains. Lapstrake planks traditionally are generally not bedded in the laps, though some builders fill open laps with paint after the boat is planked. The oil-based bedding compounds eventually dry out or leach into the wood, and it may be difficult to keep the fits tight in situations where the boat is out of the water for long periods of time. Boats that will live in the water need little bedding, as the water will swell the boat tight.

The case for polyurethane bedding revolves around the modern need to trailer our boats. Planks dry out when subjected to winds at 60 miles an hour on the freeway. This tends to favor the new adhesives, despite the drawbacks. The main reasons for needing to disassemble a boat are dry rot in the stem or the plank ends, or extensive damage caused by a collision with a solid object. Unless the boat is inadvertently built with rot-infected wood, rot will not be a problem unless the boat is neglected or improperly stored on the ground. The key to longevity is to store the boat out of the weather in a cool, dry location off the ground. In a case of a major accident, be sure you are well insured; repairs will be costly. Fortunately, with modern waterproof gap-filling glues and adhesives, many repairs can be made without the major disassembly formerly required. There is a choice to make here. I decided to use polyurethane bedding in the boat that I built, *Catherine*, as she lives on a trailer. I will discuss both methods as we move along. With a few exceptions, the construction is basically the same. The availability of modern adhesives has led to a few other changes in the construction details which I hope will simplify the building process.

Whatever technique you use, basic principles apply: Make your fits tight, wear safety gear (respirator, gloves, and hearing protection), work in a well-ventilated area, and clean up thoroughly immediately after the application of glues and adhesives.

How much time, space, and money do I need?

The Whitehall boat is a major project for an amateur builder. The time will vary from person to person. You should plan on 250 to 300 hours. If you average 8 hours per week, it will take approximately 38 weeks; let's say at least one year if you have a life.

The boat is 4 feet by 14 feet, and you need at least 5 feet all around; that is 14 feet by 24 feet, or a one-car garage. Optimally you could add 6 feet on one side for a workbench and some space to mill lumber, which would give you 20 feet by 24 feet—but in a pinch you can do with less. I will show you how to build the boat on a ladder jig. With this jig you can move the boat over as you work on each side, thus optimizing your space. I will discuss this in more detail in the next chapter on the setup.

Money will be determined by the prices you pay. In the year 2000 you might pay around $2,500 to $3,000 for materials, including sails. This cost could vary considerably. A person with good sources could get this down to under $2,000, while some could spend $3,500. This is just a very rough guess, but it should give you an idea what you are getting into.

Where do I get the materials?

The best first step is to get smart about what is available in your area. Check with maritime museums, boat schools, boatbuilders, and boat repair shops for local sources. One way to get information is through association with other amateur builders. I belong to the Traditional Small Craft Association (TSCA), which has chapters all over the country (see "Sources," in the next chapter). Price carefully before you buy. Local sources are not necessarily the best or the cheapest. I was able to buy some excellent vertical-grained red cedar for planking that originally was milled for a house deck job. I will include a few sources that will ship throughout the country. I have been amazed how many of the East Coast builders of the Heidi skiff were able to get West Coast woods. I will go into more detail on wood and other materials in the next chapter.

Boatbuilder's jargon

If you haven't already guessed, boatbuilders have a language of their own. Let's take a little time to unravel some of the gobbledegook.

Apex line—The line, inside of the rabbet, at which the inner corner of the plank strikes the stem, keel, and deadwood.

Athwartships—Running across the beam of the boat.

Batten—A thin, bendable strip of wood used to draw curves or to line out planks.

Batten (keel)—A piece of wood (⅝ inch by 2½ inches) fastened to the keel to which the garboard is screwed. The stem is fastened to the forward end of the batten.

Bead—A decorative detail routed at the bottom of the sheerstrake and/or risers.

Bearding line—The line made by the intersection of the inside of the plank with the stem, keel or keel batten, and deadwood.

Bevel—An angle sawn or planed onto a piece of wood.

Binder—In traditional Whitehall construction, the ⅝-inch-thick sheerstrake is lapped onto this ½-inch-thick cedar plank, the next plank down.

Breasthook—A piece of wood cut to fit in the angle formed by the forward end of the sheerstrakes and the stem. It is a structural member key to stiffening the boat.

Broads—The first planks after the garboard. They are usually the widest planks, so that the planks can be narrower as they turn the bilge.

Bow—The forward end of the boat at the stem.

Bucking iron—A smooth, rounded piece of steel used by auto-body repair people (they call this a *dolly*) to back up rivets and body hammering. Boatbuilders use them to back up copper rivets and nails, and tacks. I have used a sledgehammer head successfully for this job.

Chamfer—To plane off the sharp corner of a piece of wood at a 45-degree angle.

Clench-nailing—A process used to fasten lapstrake planking. A copper nail or tack is driven through a pre-drilled hole through the lapped planks. Approximately ¼" to ⅜" of the nail protrudes through the plank. As the nail is driven through the planks, a bucking iron forces the nail to bend over a small distance and then bends the point back into the plank. The nail acts like a staple.

Cove—A concave half-round rabbet routed in the gunwale.

Deadrise—The angle formed by the rise of the bottom planks and the keel.

Deadwood—A built-up section of the backbone under and just forward of the transom that fills the area that is created as the plank line rises from the deepest part of the hull to the bottom of the transom.

Fair—Description of a line that sweeps in a single direction without kinks or lumps.

Flitches—Planks cut clear across the tree lengthwise, leaving a plank with the heartwood in the center and bark on both edges.

Floor timber—A frame which crosses the keel and several planks on each side, tying together the bottom planks, the frame, and the keel.

Fore and aft (forward and after)—Toward the front and back of the boat.

Fore-and-aft—Running lengthwise along the boat.

Garboard—The plank next to the keel.

Gain (or chase in England)—A tapered channel or rabbet cut into the forward and aft edges of lapping plank faces. It is used in lapstrake planking to fit the lapped planks flush at the transom and stem.

Guardrail—Half-round rail attached to outer upper edge of the sheerstrake; also called the rubrail.

Halyard—A line used to hoist the sail.

Hardwood—Lumber cut from deciduous trees, that is, leafed trees that shed their leaves in winter (such as oak, mahogany, maple).

Hood ends—The forward ends of the planks as they fit into the stem rabbet.

Inwale—A rail that runs along the inside of the sheer, fastened over the frames.

Keel—A fore-and-aft timber on the bottom of the boat which ties the bottom planks together and gives the boat directional stability when moving through the water.

Knee—A roughly right-angled timber that is used for bracing, strengthening, and support at the intersection of structural pieces. Can be bent, laminated, or grown with a naturally curved grain.

Ladder jig—A sturdy foundation for the setup of the boat.

Lapstrake (or clinker in England)—A planking method in which planks overlap along the seams.

Lay—Direction of the twist in a rope or line.

Molds—Cross-sectional forms, set up at stations along the ladder jig, on which the boat is built.

Plain-sawn (flat-grained)—A plank sawn so that the growth rings are roughly parallel to the plank face, appearing as swirls on the surface. Pine shelving and construction lumber is cut this way.

Planking stock—Lumber selected for light weight, flexibility, and strength.

Post (or thwart stanchion)—A piece of wood used to brace up the seats. On fancy boats this is a turned piece.

Quarter knee—A piece of wood cut to fit in the angle formed by the after end of each sheerstrake and the transom. It is a structural member key to stiffening the boat.

Rabbet—The channel cut into the stem, keel, and deadwood to receive the edge of the garboard strake and the hood ends of the planks.

Rabbet line—The line made by the intersection of the outer surface of the garboard strake and the hood ends of the planks at the deadwood, keel, and stem.

Rails—Hardwood guardrails at the sheer of the boat.

Rake—Angle off of the perpendicular of the stem, transom, or mast.

Ribbands—Battens sprung around the molds. Used when carvel planking to make a jig into which the oak frames are bent. Ribbands are removed as the planks are fastened to the frames.

Riser—A fore-and-aft structural member on either side of the boat, fastened to the frames, which supports the seats.

Sheer—The top edge of the top plank at the deck or rail.

Sheerstrake—The uppermost plank, to which the rail is attached.

Sheet—A line attached to the sail which adjusts the sail's angle to the wind.

Sister floors—Floors added to back up cracked bent frames or floor timbers.

Softwood—Lumber cut from evergreen trees (cedars, spruces, pines, fir).

Spall—A piece of wood tying together the ends of the two halves of the molds.

Spline—A piece of wood cut to fit in slots cut in the edges of two planks. The spline keeps the edges of the planks aligned when glued and clamped.

Stations—The lines on the ladder jig to which the molds are set up. The stations come from the original design drawing and are part of the full-sized lofting.

Stem—A structural member at the forward end of the boat. The forward ends of the planks fasten here.

Stern—The aftermost part of the boat, where the transom is located.

Strake—A plank.

Thwart—A seat.

Transom—A planked-up area in the stern to which the after end of the planks fasten.

Tuck of the transom—The rise of the aft underside of the hull to the transom.

Turn of the bilge—The curve of the hull as it turns up from the bottom to the sheer.

Vertical-grained (quarter-sawn)—A plank cut in such a way that the growth rings are 45 to 90 degrees to the flat surface of the plank, leaving straight lines on the face of the plank.

II

Getting Started

How to use this book

This book is set up to be a step-by-step instructional manual. It is best to thoroughly read the book before beginning.

It is not a bad idea for first-timers to construct a model to get the idea of what is going on. Get an architect's scale from your local drafting supply store with a 3 inches = 1 foot scale on it (they usually have several scales on each side). Then go through the steps of the setup, lining out the planks, and fitting the garboard and one or two planks on one side. Use balsa from the model shop for planks, and Honduras mahogany or hard pine for the stem and transom. This does not have to be a museum-quality model. For my first Whitehall model I planked the whole thing, and as a result my lining-out and planking job drew an admiring response. It was well worth the effort. The scale of 3 inches = 1 foot is large enough that you can use your smaller shop tools (once you learn how to make them sharp!).

For building the full-sized Whitehall, I have tried to estimate the amount of materials you will need, but it is best that you make your own estimates as you go, as you may be buying a variety of dimensions. Always keep a good variety of screws on hand, as you might use different-size screws than I did. You are the boss. What looks good probably is good. The illustrations are not to scale, so use the printed measurements.

Organizing your shop

We have discussed your space requirements in the first chapter. Basically we need at least the equivalent of a one-car garage. It is important that the layout be as efficient as possible. Here are some considerations.

Wall space is always at a premium. Doors and windows break up the space and limit the kind of activity that can take place. Before you go out and spend a lot of money on workbenches and floor tools, it is a good idea to take a look at your requirements and lay out where the tools, benches, and lumber storage will be. Don't clutter up the shop with stuff you won't use.

Lumber storage is best on racks above the doors and windows along the long walls; this gets it out of the way. If your shop is heated, you don't want to store wood for long periods inside, as it will over-dry. In that case, an unheated building or a sheltered area outside will be best. For longer-term outside storage, the planks should be stored off the ground in layers. Each layer should be separated with narrow pieces of wood (called *stickers*) at least ¾ inch thick and the same space between the plank edges so that air can circulate evenly around each plank. Just be careful to protect this stack from wind, weather, and temperature extremes.

The most useful floor tools are a 14-inch bandsaw with an edge guide and mounted on wheels for mobility, and a 12-inch portable planer. You can get by with these tools alone. Next most useful is a table saw. In a small shop a table saw can take up a lot of room, but I have seen some good-looking 10-inch portable table saws. When the saw is not in use you can store it in another area. Some sort of dust-collection setup is important. The planer can generate mountains of chips and dust. At the end of this chapter I will list some tool companies that sell this stuff.

Benches are a problem in a small shop, as they take up space and often act as a catchall for miscellaneous tools. Boats make specialized demands on workbenches. My favorite workbench is the Black & Decker Workmate, as it is designed to clamp long pieces like planks. You can work around it and can fold it out of the way when you are not using it. A small, shallow workbench against the wall with a metal vise, bench grinder, small drill press, and woodworker's vise is good addition.

When I am gluing up transoms and assembling the stem, I like to have a deeper bench that I can get around. I make up a temporary bench out of two saw horses and a lightweight hollow-core door. When I am done with my project, I can take this bench apart and store it away. Remember to design-in shelves wherever they fit for tools, fittings, parts, paints and goos, extension chords, and fastenings. I never have enough space, so I have become a space miser!

Hand tools

This is a short list of most of the hand tools you might need. Some you might dispense with if you figured out alternatives, and you might want to buy other tools not on the list. It's up to you to decide what is best.

6-inch block plane (20- and/or 11-degree angle)

9½-inch smoothing plane

10-inch rabbet plane (Stanley duplex type with edge guide)

18-inch fore plane, or 14-inch jack plane

3-inch trim plane

Adjustable spokeshave (with screw adjusters)

Chisels—¼, ½, ⅝, and ¾ inch. Carpenter's butt chisels are not the best, but will work. You will need at least one longer-bladed woodworker's chisel. If you can only afford one, buy a ½-inch or ⅝-inch size.

Various screwdrivers (that fit tightly into the slots of the screws you are using)

File—medium-cut half-round and round

2⅜-inch hole saw (hand drill attachment—for sailing rig)

Heavy-duty scissors

16-ounce carpenter's hammer

Small ball-peen hammer

2-pound hammer head or equivalent—for bucking tacks or clench nails

Hand drill—⅜-inch chuck (12–14-volt cordless with clutch and extra battery pack if you can afford it)

Handsaw (10-point or medium-tooth equivalent Japanese pull saw)

Dovetail saw (or equivalent fine-tooth Japanese pull saw)

Level—carpenter's type (mine is 2 feet long; anything close to this is fine)

Pencil sharpener

Pencils—#3 to #6 artist type

Pencil eraser—white (from drafting store)

1½-inch putty knife

Sabersaw (also called jigsaw) with metal cutting blades

Sharpening stones—grits 250, 600–800, 1,200, 6,000–8,000

Router (optional, at least 1½ horsepower) with assorted carbide cutters (½-, ⅜-, ¼-, and ⅛-inch quarter-round; ¼-inch beading)

Measuring tools—16-foot tape measure, combination square, level, 24-by-16-inch steel carpenter's square

Drills and countersinks—for #8, #10, #12, and #14 wood screws

Assorted clamps (minimum numbers)

C-clamps, six 6-inch and/or 4-inch

Spring clamps, four to six 4-inch (for rails)

Pipe clamps, three at least 2½ feet long

Wooden cabinet clamps or cam clamps, six 6 to 8 inches deep (cam clamps, shown in Figure 31A, are best for clamping plank laps

Caulking gun—common hardware-store variety (for tubes of polyurethane bedding compound); get a heavy-duty one

Safety equipment

Respirator with filters for dust and solvent fumes

Hearing protection (industrial grade)

Safety glasses with side shields

Latex or vinyl surgical gloves (box of 100)

Paper towels (for cleanup)

waterproof/heat resistant gloves for steambending

Wood

Fine wooden boats have been built everywhere of local or imported wood. Do your homework at nearby boatshops, maritime museums, and repair yards to learn about local sources. *WoodenBoat* magazine is a good source of information.

On the west coast of the United States quantities of lumber are cut from large trees. The lumber is carefully sized and graded, and shipped all over the country. Most of this stuff is softwood (wood cut from evergreen trees). The most common softwoods available are Douglas-fir, Western red cedar, Alaska yellow cedar, Sitka spruce, and Port Orford cedar. The best of these for lapstrake planking are red cedar and Port Orford cedar. You should be able to find them locally, but in a pinch, the suppliers in the source list at the end of this chapter will ship anywhere.

Yellow cedar is not recommended, as it is prone to split, though it is sometimes used. Sitka spruce is the best for spars and oars, though I have used it for planking as well. It is not a particularly rot-resistant wood, so a boat planked with spruce will not last long if neglected. Another West Coast wood seen in lumberyards is ponderosa pine, commonly sold for shelving. It is too susceptible to rot to use for boat wood, but is great for molds. On the East Coast, Eastern spruce is available, and I am told it is cheaper as well. Fir is a good substitute for hardwoods for stems, transoms, and keels, as it is as strong as oak yet much lighter and more stable. It is a little too stiff and heavy for planking. Any of these woods are good for floorboards and seats, as they are strong and light.

White cedar (Eastern white cedar, grown in the Northeast, and Atlantic white cedar, grown in the southeast United States) is the favorite of the old-time Northeast boatbuilders and comes highly recommended by those who use it. White cedar usually comes ungraded, so the purchaser has to select out suitable stock. The trees it is cut from are small, and the sawmill cuts it in plain-sawn *flitches*—planks cut clear through the tree, leaving the heartwood in the center and bark on both edges. White cedar also has knots, which add structure to the plank if small and tight, but must be glued in or removed and plugged if large.

Common hardwoods are red oak, white oak, and Honduras mahogany. Of the oaks, white oak is preferred, as it is less prone to rot—although oak as a class is not noted for its rot resistance. Oak is prized for boatbuilding, as it is available in large quantities and usually reasonably priced. In many places it is cut locally, and large quantities are shipped out of Oregon and the southeastern United States. Oak is a dense, tough, resilient wood that holds fastenings well and is excellent for steam-bending. Its drawbacks are that it is heavy and is hard to paint and glue. However, modern adhesives such as polyurethanes will stick to just about anything. In small boats like this Whitehall, I like to restrict its use to the frames, the keel batten, and rails because of its weight.

Honduras mahogany is the favorite of boat-builders as well as cabinet and furniture makers. It is reasonably priced and commonly available everywhere. It can be used everywhere in a boat except frames, as it is not a great wood for steaming. It glues and holds fastenings well and, when varnished and exposed to sunlight, darkens to a deep, rich brown. I like it especially for the transom, stem, keel, and deadwood.

Ordering wood

When ordering wood, it is important to specify how the wood is cut. As a rule, clear, knot-free wood is more stable (less susceptible to cupping and splitting) when it is cut so that the growth rings are from 45 to 90 degrees to the face of the plank. This lumber is called *vertical-grained, rift,* or *quarter-sawn*, and the grain appears as straight lines on the face of the plank. Douglas-fir, red cedar, Sitka spruce, and usually Port Orford cedar are purchased this way. When the plank is cut so that the growth rings are roughly parallel to the face, it is called *flat-grained* or *plain-sawn*. The grain appears as oval swirls on the face of the plank. Most hardwoods, planking stock with tight knots, and mold stock are ordered this way.

Wood is sold by the board foot—that is, 1 foot by 1 foot by 1 inch thick, rough. Any finishing cost is added to the price. You pay for all the planer chips and sawdust! The actual cost you will pay for your wood is determined by the amount of wood you use plus what you throw out. The key here is to buy efficiently, even if it might cost a bit more. Buying at a lower price planks that are wider or longer than you need can lead to additional cost. Figure your costs as the amount of wood purchased per finished plank plus shipping and tax.

Most wood is graded before it is cut, and the price is determined by the quality of the grade. In some situations, the stock may be ungraded or of a low grade that requires you to select out suitable boat lumber. This will require knowledge of available local wood and the characteristics required of each species. White cedar is most likely to be sold this way. West Coast cedars are all graded. Most of the time, if the salesman is knowledgeable and you explain the purpose you intend to use the wood for, he will steer you to the right grade. These grades usually tell you how knot-free the plank is. There is usually a certain amount of below-grade stock allowed. A reputable dealer will guarantee the grade and replace anything that doesn't measure up. It is always wise to inspect the wood yourself if you can. Many times, by necessity, planks are graded at the mill one side, one edge, so who knows what you will find on the other side. Vertical-grain, C or better, is the common minimum for West Coast cedar boat planking and fir for stems, transoms, and the keel. Higher grades will cost more.

Even clear planks can have *spike knots*, knots formed by the roots of branches as they penetrate the trunk of the tree. Spike knots cause hard-to-see swirls in the grain for some distance around the branch root. They can cut at a sharp angle across the plank. In a 5/16-inch plank, this can fatally weaken the plank. Check the edges of the rough planking stock carefully. The swirls from the spike knots will show up as rough spots running counter to the general run of the grain of rough-cut lumber.

There are a few more things you should know before you try to order wood. Wood is sized by the quarter inch in rough thickness (four quarters, designated as 4/4, equals 1 inch) and by inches in rough width. Quite often it is sized in 2-inch increments in widths over 4 inches, and 2-foot increments in lengths over 8 feet. The builder is usually expected to purchase the wood rough and then have it milled to his specifications. Milling will consist of resawing and/or surfacing. If the planks are sold surfaced, they are designated S2S (surfaced two sides).

Green or uncured wood will cup, bend, twist, and split and be unusable. Before wood can be used for building boats, the moisture content of the wood must be equalized with the moisture in the air where you are going to build your boat. There are two drying methods used to accomplish this: *kiln-drying* and *air-drying*. Boatbuilders prefer air-drying, as it allows the moisture to slowly evaporate without unnecessarily stressing or over-drying the wood. This method also preserves the resins, which are rot-resistant and, when combined with the moisture content in the plank, give the plank good bending characteristics. The rough planks are stored outside (not indoors in a heated environment) off the ground and separated by stickers, narrow strips of wood about the same thickness of the plank. The planks are stacked with about the same separation edgewise as well. These stacks are covered to protect them from rain and wind. Depending on the species, air-drying six to eight months is usually enough. Boatbuilders like the wood to be cut in the early spring whenever possible, as this is when the sap is down. This aids the drying process by naturally eliminating some of the moisture content.

Kiln-drying is a controversial subject. Many of the hardwoods are dried this way. Air-drying is too expensive for large lumber dealers, so they resort to drying the wood quickly in a kiln. If the wood is not over-dried or dried too quickly, it may survive this process. Some woods are only surface-dried to prevent damage during shipping and storage at the lumberyard. This is the best option. In many places in the country there may be no choice—what you see is what you get. In any case, always sticker the wood for a while to acclimate it to your area.

Planking should always be air-dried. This thin softwood stock dries out quickly and will split easily if over-dried. If necessary, ship it in from a reliable supplier of boat lumber. Bending oak for frames should also be green, not dried. I have used dried wood for this, and I assure you that although it may work sometimes, it's not worth the trouble. Bending oak many times is not sold at a premium, so ship it in if you must.

When ordering planking stock for this boat, I might order 8/4 planks of vertical-grain, C or better, Western red cedar 6 inches wide, 16 feet long. I can get three finished ⁵⁄₁₆-inch planks out of each rough plank, so to get eighteen finished planks, I ordered six rough planks. Normally I would find a local woodworking shop with a resaw bandsaw to get three ½-inch rough planks out of my 8/4 stock, since my small 14-inch bandsaw can't handle that deep a cut. However, I was able to cut this on my table saw by first cutting on one edge, and then turning it over and cutting through the other edge; the small amount left in the middle of each cut I could saw with the bandsaw. By using 6-inch-wide stock I saved the cost of resawing, at the expense of having to scarf a few planks. After I had my rough ½-inch planks, I planed them on my portable planer to ⁵⁄₁₆ inch. You have to make sure that the lumber salesman is selling you a full 8/4, as some fudge on this. You have to know what the width of the resaw cut (kerf) will be and how much to plane off. Allow a minimum of ¹⁄₁₆ inch of wood to plane off each surface of each plank and usually ⅛ inch for each kerf. That means you will lose ¼ inch to the kerf and ⅜ inch to the surfacing. That should leave you a little for any extra surfacing required by a rough saw cut, and you'll still get three planks out of an 8/4 plank. A large mill might require ³⁄₁₆ inch for kerf, so you would have to adjust accordingly. The millwright will tell you what his kerf is.

Hardwoods can be had surfaced or rough. The keel, stem, and deadwood can be bought at 1½ inch or 6/4 rough if available. You will finish it to 1⅜ inch, so this will save you the cost of buying 8/4 and planing off ½ inch of costly hardwood. Rails, transom, keel batten, and seats are purchased 4/4, and the six floorboards are resawn out of two 8/4 planks.

Most boatbuilders become skillful scroungers. The cost of wood encourages this pastime. For my *Catherine* I found excellent vertical-grained red cedar planking stock disguised as house-building material. It was half the price of the stuff the boat lumber suppliers sell. For seats, keels, deadwood, stems, transoms, or for that matter, almost anything except framing or planking, lack of width of the stock can be made up by edge-gluing with epoxy. This allows the scrounger to "high-grade" construction-grade lumber stacks. I have lived in a town full of boatbuilders where, if you wanted to get the high grade, you had to know someone at the lumberyard so you could get there first. Always be courteous and restack the lumber piles carefully. Some lumberyards or mills high-grade their own stock and sell the result as "pull-outs." I have bought green old-growth fir 2-by-4s (milled 1½ inches by 3½ inches for house studs) this way, air-dried it, and glued it up for all kinds of boat parts, including spars and oars. Seats can be glued up out of vertical-grained red cedar decking.

Unfortunately, the vertical-grained fir commonly sold at the lumberyards for cabinet and finish work has most of the time been excessively kiln-dried, which makes it stiff, brittle, and rot-prone. However, in a pinch it can be used for seats where it will be well ventilated, and can be replaced if necessary. The stiffness is an asset, and its brittle nature can be overcome by carefully pre-drilling the screw holes.

Fastenings

Bronze screws and bolts are the fastenings of choice of the traditional boatbuilder. Stainless will do but tends to be more expensive. For clench-nailing these small boats, I prefer copper tacks over clench nails. Tacks are cheaper as they come more to the pound, and clench nails often are to hard to give a good clench without *annealing* them first (heating them up and allowing a slow cooling to soften them up). It is hard to lean under a boat holding a bucking iron over the point of the fastening while trying to tap on the head with a hammer. The long, thin point of the tack bends easier and holds just fine. I have specified 1-inch tacks, although ideally ⅞-inch would be better for this boat. They just don't make them that way. The ideal length protruding through the plank should be 3⁄16 to ¼ inch. You can cut off the ends of any tacks that are too long.

In traditional construction, most builders rely on bolts or heavy copper rivets to fasten together the stem assembly, and drift pins (bronze rod with a point on one end and a peened-over head on the other) in the deadwood and sternpost assemblies. These heavy fastenings are used because, without adhesives, they are the only things holding the parts together. Nowadays, with adhesives like epoxy and polyurethane, long #14 screws can be substituted in the stem. The construction plan for this boat eliminates the need for drift pins in the deadwood. It should be noted that when gluing oak, polyurethanes are preferable, as there have been reports of occasional failures with epoxy. Oak has long had a reputation of being difficult to glue. I don't use oak where I need structural glue joints, and that takes care of the problem.

Tool sharpening

Before anyone attempts to build a boat or any fine woodworking project, they must learn to properly sharpen hand tools. This is a relatively simple task. Unfortunately, most people are confounded by poorly sharpened hand tools. They then turn to power tools and use the blades until they smoke. When building small wooden boats, sharp tools are a must, so let's get to it.

I have used many different sharpening systems over the years. I started out with Arkansas oil stones, migrated to Japanese water stones, and ended up with diamond stones. All use oil or water to keep the filings from becoming embedded in the stone and clogging it up. Arkansas oil stones work great and leave a fine film of oil on your tools which preserves them as it helps lubricate the cutting action. Eventually, however, if used a lot, these stones lose their flat surface and are difficult to flatten again. Japanese water stones also work well and are reasonably priced. They are soft and lose their flatness quickly, but can be flattened easily with 250-grit wet-or-dry sandpaper on a machined flat surface like a table saw or even a piece of thick glass. The stones have to be kept in water, which can be a pain. The diamond stones are my favorite, as they stay flat and can be used to sharpen carbide router bits. Water is used as the lubricant. Diamond stones, naturally, are the most expensive. They are made by embedding diamond dust into a steel surface. I have three grits: 250-grit for rough grinding, 600-grit for all-purpose sharpening, and 1,200-grit for final surfacing. For fine work such as for carving, this edge might be finished on a 5,000-grit water stone, or honed with brass polish rubbed onto a leather strop. Stores that sell fine woodworking tools sell a variety of strops and honing material, but I just like to make do with stuff I find around the shop. If your budget is tight, the minimum requirement is a 600-grit stone. A woodcarver friend of mine, who maintains his tools at a much higher level than most boatbuilders, uses 600-grit wet-or-dry sandpaper set on the flat surface of his table saw. His carving knives have a variety of shapes. He wraps the 600-grit paper over an axe handle, which has all the curves he needs to sharpen his tools. He then hones with brass polish (he has a favorite brand) rubbed on a piece of surfaced but untreated leather.

When buying new planes and chisels, the first thing you must do is make sure that the back of the blade is flat. You can do this by holding the back of the blade flat on the 600-grit stone and working it in a circular motion. After a brief while, check the back of the blade. If the scratches go clear across the back along the edge, it is flat. If not, keep working it until it is.

Sometimes you buy a used tool that has been misused and the edge is chewed up. This is just fine since the person who sells it to you thinks the tool is worthless and you should get it for next to nothing. All that is needed to get it up and running is to flatten the back and grind a 25-degree bevel on the edge, and you are good as new. Most people just estimate this angle, but those who demand precision can buy gauges to check the angle. To hold the angle while using the sharpening stone, you can buy guides to hold the blade while you sharpen. They are inexpensive and work well. The old-timers, with some practice, learn to hold this angle by hand. However, eventually the edge rounds over, requiring the grinding of a new edge. With a guide this step should not be required. Some people like to grind the beveled edge to a 30-degree angle and then sharpen the edge to 25 degrees, thus limiting the amount of sharpening required to renew the edge. This is called a *micro bevel*. This is not required if you use the guide and touch up the edge regularly.

Grinding on a stone, even a 250-grit stone, can be time-consuming. If you want to keep the temper of your blade, this is probably the most prudent method. Most folks use a bench grinder with an 80-grit wheel. Don't use anything finer, as it will overheat the steel quickly. After each pass, they plunge the blade into a can filled with water to keep the blade cool. You can buy wheels that do not heat up as much as the standard carborundum wheels. This process is repeated until a hollow is created with the radius of the wheel which encompasses the whole bevel. There will also be a curled feather edge, called a *burr* or wire edge. The next step will remove this.

The sharpening process is simple. Once the back is flattened and the proper angle is established, use the 600-grit stone until the scratches are even across the edge. At this point you will see that there is a burr on the edge. To remove the burr, turn the blade over to the flat and work it a few times, then back to the beveled edge again. Repeat this process until the burr disappears. If all you have is a 600-grit stone, this will work fine.

At each grit, the scratches on your edge get finer and finer. There is no need to use each grit further once the scratches are uniform. A 600-grit edge works well for planes and most rough chisel work, but most boatbuilders are finicky and like to get a finer edge. I like to go to a 1,200-grit stone. At this grit there is virtually no burr. For chisels, I like to hone the edge after sharpening.

Once you have a good edge, you must periodically maintain it. A dull edge has a shine along it when you hold it up to the light; this is called the *candle*. A sharp edge does not reflect light.

Materials list

Hopefully the quantities are generous enough to allow for errors. There may be local woods that could be substituted. As you get to each section, review the materials list to ensure that the quantities are enough for the job. Fastenings are approximate; it is a good idea to have a stock of different-size screws on hand to choose from.

Wood

Ladder jig— three construction-grade 2 by 4s (net 1½ inches by 3½ inches, dry, straight), 16 feet long.

Molds—pine, shelving-quality S4S (sided four sides); four pieces 1 inch by 12 inches rough, 12 feet long (¾ inch by 11½ inches finished).

Mold cross spalls—pine, shelving-quality S4S; three pieces 1 inch by 4 inches rough, 12 feet long (13/16 inch by 3½ inches finished).

Keel—Honduras mahogany, fir, white oak; one piece 1⅜ inches by 1½ inches, 13 feet long.

Keel batten—white oak; one piece ⅝ inch by 2½ inches, 13 feet long.

Transom—Honduras mahogany, fir; one piece 13/16 inch by 7 inches, 9 feet long.

Stem, transom knee, deadwood, maststep— Honduras mahogany, fir, white oak; one piece 1⅜ inches by 8 inches, 8 feet long.

Fairing battens—⅝ inch by ⅝ inch, 16 feet long (finished dimensions), from two pieces of clear softwood stock 13/16 inch by 5½ inches, 16 feet long.

Planking—eighteen pieces white cedar flitches, or red or Port Orford cedar, 5/16 inch by 6 inches, 16 feet long (can be resawn from six pieces 8/4 by 6 inches, 16 feet long, rough).

Quarter knees, thwart knees, breasthook, tiller— Honduras mahogany, fir, white oak; one piece 13/16 inch by 8 inches, 6 feet long.

Frames (allowing for 25 percent breakage)—flat-grained, green, clear white oak bending stock; four pieces 4/4 by 7 inches, 8 feet long (to net at least 25 frames ⅝ inch on the flat by ¾ inch; you will need 19 for the boat plus extras for breakage). You can get this from a local mill if you have the experience to select out the best stock or if someone is available to help you. Otherwise, you may be better off ordering the frame stock from a reliable source.

Rails—Honduras mahogany, fir, white oak; one piece ⅝ inch by 6 inches, 16 feet long.

Seat risers—Honduras mahogany, fir, white oak; one piece ⅝ inch by 8 inches, 11 feet long.

Floorboards—same wood as planking; four pieces 5⁄16 inch by 6 inches, 11 feet long (six pieces can be resawn out of two pieces 8/4 by 6 inches, 12 feet long, rough; you might need the extra planks to replace planks that you break or crack).

Daggerboard case sides—6-millimeter (¼-inch) Honduras mahogany marine plywood; 1 foot by 2 feet.

Daggerboard case posts and bedlogs—mahogany, fir (one piece ¾ inch by 5⁄8 inch by 4 feet).

Daggerboard—fir, ½ inch by 8 inches, 3 feet long; or two laminations of 6-millimeter (¼-inch) Honduras mahogany marine plywood.

Thwarts, stern seat, mast partner—white cedar, red cedar, Port Orford cedar, fir (keep this lightweight); two pieces ¾ inch by 9 inches (8 and 7 inches finished), 14 feet and 12 feet long.

Turned posts—two, made of 1½-inch by 1½-inch by 9-inch stock. Can be bought at a home-improvement store, or you can turn yourself on a lathe (or shape them with a rasp and chisel).

Backrest (optional)—Honduras mahogany, ¾ inch by 9½ inches, 34 inches long.

Traditional rudder—¾-inch mahogany marine plywood (can be glued up from three laminations of 6-millimeter mahogany marine plywood), 2 feet by 3 feet.

Tiller—oak or mahogany, ¾ inch by 4 feet by 1½ inches.

Kick-up rudder—one-half sheet 6-millimeter mahogany marine plywood.

Gaff (for lugsail)—spruce or fir; 6/4 by 6/4 rough, 8 feet long (1½ inches by 1½ inches finished).

Sprit (for spritsail)—spruce or fir; 6/4 by 6/4 rough, 12 feet long (1½ inches by 1½ inches finished).

Boom (both rigs)—spruce or fir; 6/4 by 6/4, by 12 feet long (finished 1½ inches by 1½ inches).

Mast (both rigs)—spruce or fir; one piece rough 5/4 or 6/4, by 5 inches, 12 feet long (make two pieces S4S 1 inch by 2 inches, 12 feet long).

Oars—spruce or fir; one piece 8/4 by 6 inches rough, 8 feet long.

Fastenings and fittings

Drywall (sheetrock) screws, steel, self-tapping—1¼-inch, 1 pound; 2½-inch, ½ pound (for molds, ladder jig, and steam box).

Clench fastenings—1-inch copper tacks, 1½ pounds (approximate); or 7⁄8-inch clench nails, 3 pounds (approximate).

Bronze wood screws (approximate; have on hand an assortment for contingencies)—¾-inch #8, 100; 1-inch #8, 600; 1¼-inch #8, 150; 1½-inch #8, 100; 1¾-inch #8, 100; 1-inch #10, 8; 2-inch, #10, 30; 2½-inch #10, 10; 1¾-inch #12 (for stem), 4; 3½-inch #14 (for stem), 4.

Bronze wood screws—four 3-inch #1 (stem fastenings, if using polyurethane bedding).

Bronze bolts—four 5⁄16-inch, 5 inches long, with nuts and washers (stem fastenings, if using traditional method).

Pan-head screws, stainless-steel, self-tapping—5⁄8-inch #6, 18 (for installing rope fender, if desired).

Carriage bolt, bronze or stainless-steel—one approximately ¼-inch, 1 inch long, with wingnut and washer (for kick-up rudder).

Machine bolts, bronze—two 2¼-inch #8, with nuts and washers, for upper pintles; two 1¼-inch #8, with nuts and washers, for lower pintles.

Brass (or bronze) fittings—two pairs oarlocks; gudgeons and pintles, one set each for ¾-inch rudder; ¼-inch by 4-inch eyebolt for trailer; 5⁄8-inch half-oval, 3 feet long (for stem band); 3⁄32-inch by 1-inch strap, 12 feet long (for keel shoe).

PVC pipe—23⁄8 inches inside diameter, 1 feet 6 inches long (for mast tube).

Drain plug—one, plastic.

Oar leathers—3⁄32- to 1⁄8-inch bridle leather, two pieces 8½ by 8 inches, two pieces 1 inch by 18 inches.

Cordage

Whipping twine—size 4 waxed polyester, one roll (for whipping running rigging); size 16 waxed polyester, one roll (for whipping rope fender).

Tarred marline—one roll (for lashing fairleads).

Nylon rope—3⁄8-inch three-strand, 40 feet (for sheet and bow line); ¼-inch three-strand, 70 feet (for sail lashing, snotter, and traveler); 5⁄8-inch three-strand, 20 feet (for rope fender, if desired).

Adhesives and caulking

Traditional method—caulking cotton (cotton plumber's wicking used to be available; you could substitute cotton string, or make your own by dividing strands of caulking cotton); oil-based caulking compound, 1 quart; oil-based bedding compound (available at marine stores), 1 quart.

Polyurethane method—polyurethane bedding compound (two such products are 3M 4200 and Sikaflex 231), white, three tubes.

Carpenter's glue—yellow, water-resistant, 1 pint.

Epoxy adhesive—1-pint kit; try for a 1-to-1 mix ratio (otherwise, be sure to get measuring cups).

Plastic wrapping tape (clear type used to wrap packages)—one roll (for protecting clamping jigs from getting glued to the assemblies).

Contact cement—½ pint (for oar leathers).

Paint, varnish, and supplies

Marine enamel or high-quality oil-based enamel—1 quart primer; 3 quarts finish paint (1 quart each for the outside, the inside, and for contrasting floorboards and seats).

Paint additive (brushing liquid)—1 quart penetrol (to make paint flow and reduce brush drag without excessive thinning).

Spar varnish, with ultraviolet filter—1 pint, for spars, transom, and rails (varnish more if you can't resist, but remember that this increases maintenance; it sure does look good, though!).

Thinners—1 gallon paint thinner (for paint and brush cleanup); 1 quart lacquer thinner (for polyurethane bedding cleanup; stove alcohol, also known as denatured alcohol, works too).

Wood filler—exterior, 1 pint.

Paintbrushes—china bristle, minimum of 2-inch, 1½-inch, and 1-inch widths.

Paper towels—three rolls (for cleanup).

Sandpaper—aluminum oxide, 80-, 100-, and 150-grit; 220-grit wet-and-dry.

Steam box

Box sides—two pieces construction-grade fir, pine, or hemlock, 2 inches by 6 inches (1½ by 5½ inches, finished) by 8 feet long; ⅜-inch C/D exterior plywood or 1-inch by 6-inch tight-knot cedar, fir, or pine, 8 feet long (see Chapter V, Figure 51).

Box interior rack—hardwood dowel, ½ inch by 3 feet long (to keep the frames up off the bottom of the box).

Steam source—25-cubic-foot propane tank and hose; cast-iron burner, crab cooker, grass burner, camp stove (or equivalent); 5-gallon metal gasoline can, or any other steel container of a similar size with a small opening; 6-inch to 1-foot rubber hot-water (auto heater) hose to fit in the can opening.

Drafting and lofting equipment

Table—two 36-inch hollow-core doors, supported on three saw horses 30 inches high (if you have limited space, you can use store-bought sawhorse clamps that allow disassembly of the saw horses).

Drafting film—Mylar, polyethylene, or vellum, 30 inches by 9 feet (I prefer Mylar or polyethylene, as the plastic resists moisture and is tougher; but heavy white kraft paper works too, if you can keep it from getting damp).

Drawing tools—black permanent-ink (for Mylar or polyethylene) .05-line felt-tip pens, from drafting supply store; #3 to #6 pencils for drafting film and paper.

Erasers—white rubber (for pencils) or yellow ink erasers (for permanent-ink felt-tip pens), from drafting supply store.

Drafting batten—¼ inch by ⅜ inch, 5 feet long, of polycarbonate (Lexan), available from stores that supply glass. Have the shopkeeper cut it from a larger sheet. It is sometimes available ready-made at drafting stores. You can use a thin piece of wood, but polycarbonate strips work much better. Drafting stores also sell a plastic batten called an "adjustable spline" that works well. Also useful is a set of ship's curves, a collection of interconnected plastic splines that can be bent to fair curves and hold them.

Various rulers—4-foot aluminum (from hardware store); steel carpenter's square; 18-to 24-inch steel ruler (from drafting supply store).

Drafting dots—round pieces of easy-to-remove masking tape, used to hold down the Mylar or vellum to your table (from drafting supply store). You can get easy-to-remove masking tape that works as well, such as the blue tape sold by 3M.

Finish nails—light-gauge, ½ pound (for battens).

Awl or push-pins—to push through the drafting film.

Ball of string—for checking the ladder jig.

Template material—one-and-a-half sheets of ⅛-inch untempered Masonite or the equivalent; two sheets poster board (from the art store).

Safety gear

Industrial-strength hearing protection for everyone in the shop.

Respirator with combination dust and vapor filters (no paper, please).

Latex or vinyl gloves, 1 box (100).

Wrap-around safety glasses or goggles.

Waterproof/heat resistant gloves for steambending

Sources

This is a short list. Ask around locally and price everything. If you can't find what you need, these people can do it for you. They ship anywhere in the USA.

Tools and Hardware

Grizzly Imports
2406 Reach Road
Williamsport, PA 17701
800-523-4777
800-541-5537
(Bellingham, WA, store)
www.grizzly.com
Low-cost floor tools, hand tools; catalog available.

Woodcraft
210 Wood County Industrial Park
P.O. Box 1686
Parkersburg, WV 26102-1686
800-225-1153
Catalog available; branches throughout the USA.

Woodworker's Supply, Inc.
1108 North Glenn Road
Casper, WY 82601
800-645-9292
Tools, beading router bits; catalog available.

The WoodenBoat Store
Naskeag Road, P.O. Box 78
Brooklin, ME 04616-9988
800-273-7447
www.woodenboat.com
Tools, books; catalog available.

Wood

Flounder Bay Boat Lumber
1019 Third Street
Anacortes, WA 92221
800-228-4691
email: boatkit@sos.net
www.flounderbay.com
Wood, fastenings, hardware, tools, books.

M. L. Condon
260 Ferris Avenue
White Plains, NY 10603
914-946-4111
All varieties of lumber.

Sails

Nathaniel Wilson
Lincoln Street, P.O. Box 71
East Boothbay, ME 04544
207- 633-5071

Bohndell Sails
US Route 1
PO Box 628
Rockport, ME 04856
Tel: 207-236-3549

Ullman Sails
Northwest 6319 Seaview Ave., N.W.
Seattle, WA 98107-2664
206-789-2171

Booksellers

Mystic Seaport Store
75 Greenmanville Avenue
Mystic, CT 06355
800-331-2665
www.mysticseaport.org

The WoodenBoat Store
Naskeag Road, P.O. Box 78
Brooklin, ME 04616-9988
800-273-7447
www.woodenboat.com

Organizations

The Center for Wooden Boats
1010 Valley Street
Seattle, WA 98109
206-382-BOAT

Mystic Seaport Watercraft Plans Collection
Mystic Seaport Museum Inc.
P.O. Box 6000
Mystic, CT 06355-0990

The Traditional Small Craft Association (TSCA)
P.O. Box 350
Mystic, CT 06355

In the United Kingdom:
Robbins Timber
Brookgate
Ashton Vale Trading Estate
Bristol BS3 2UN
England
0117 963 3136
fax: 0117 963 7927
email: timber@robbins.co.uk
www.robbins.co.uk

Davey & Co London Ltd
1, Chelmsford Road Industrial Estate
Great Dunmow
Essex CMG 1HD
England
01371 876361
email: chandlery@davey.co.uk

III

Setting Up

The setup is a critical step in building your boat. It determines the shape of the boat and provides the base for your boat-building efforts. It has to be accurate, fair (no lumps, flat spots, or unwanted twists), and sturdy, yet light enough to move around if required. Don't rush here. My instructions include steps to check your setup as you go, so please, no short-cuts. Completely read through this section and study the illustrations carefully. Understand completely what you are about to do before you cut any wood. Careful preparation eliminates errors and speeds up the work. Speed is gained by getting it right the first time. There is an old boat-builder's saying that applies here: "Check twice, cut once."

Materials required

Jig (see Figure 2)

Ladder jig—construction-grade 2 by 4s, dry and straight; two pieces 14 feet 5½ inches long, two pieces 15 inches long, seven pieces 18 inches long.

Molds, transom braces, and gussets—shelving pine, plain-sawn, tight-knot, ¾ inch by 11½ inches; four pieces, 12 feet long.

Cross spalls—three pieces, 3½ inches wide, 12 feet long.

Drywall (sheetrock) screws—1¼-inch, ½ pound; 2½-inch, ½ pound.

Fairing battens—⅝ inch by ⅝ inch by 16 feet; order two pieces of clear pine ¹³⁄₁₆ inch by 5½ inches, 16 long.

- **Materials required**
- **Your workspace**
- **Draft and build the stem assembly**
- **Build the molds**
- **Shape the transom**
- **Cut out and assemble the backbone**
- **Build the daggerboard case**
- **Build the ladder jig**
- **Set up the backbone and the molds**
- **Check the rabbet and transom bevels**
- **Line out the planks**

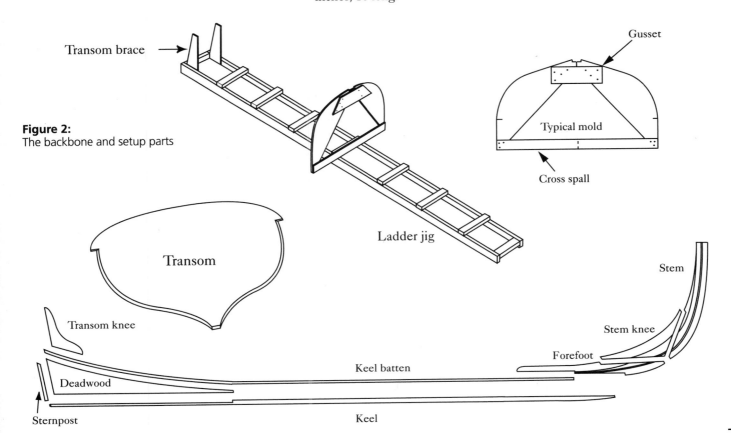

Figure 2:
The backbone and setup parts

Transom brace

Gusset

Typical mold

Cross spall

Ladder jig

Transom

Transom knee

Stem

Stem knee

Forefoot

Deadwood

Keel batten

Sternpost

Keel

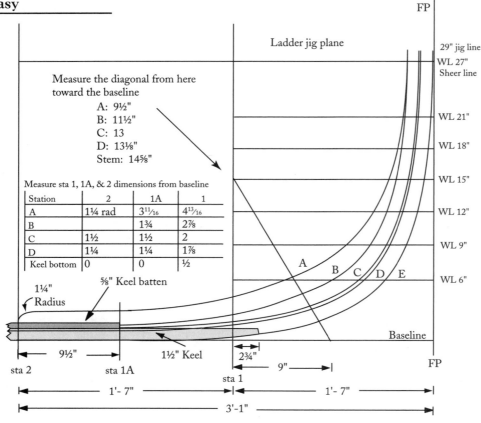

Measure the diagonal from here toward the baseline

- A: 9½"
- B: 11½"
- C: 13
- D: 13⅛"
- Stem: 14⅝"

Measure sta 1, 1A, & 2 dimensions from baseline

Station	2	1A	1
A	1¼ rad	3¹¹/₁₆	4¹³/₁₆
B		1¾	2⅞
C	1½	1½	2
D	1¼	1¼	1⅞
Keel bottom	0	0	½

1¼" Radius

⅝" Keel batten

9½" 1½" Keel 2¾" 9"

sta 2   sta 1A   sta 1

1'- 7"   1'- 7"

3'-1"

Figure 3:
Stem and keel dimensions

Note: All measurements at A, B, C, D, and E are distances from FP in inches

WL	A	B	C	D	E
29"	2⅛	2⅛	1⁹/₁₆	1⁷/₁₆	0
27"	2⅛	2⅛	1½	1⁷/₁₆	0
21"	2⅝	2½	1⅞	1¾	¼
18"	3⁵/₁₆	2¹⁵/₁₆	2¼	2⅛	⁹/₁₆
15"	4⅜	3¹¹/₁₆	2⅞	2¾	1³/₁₆
12"	6³/₁₆	5	3⅞	3¾	2⅛
9"	9⅜	7³/₁₆	5½	5⅜	3⁹/₁₆
6"	14⅞	10⅝	8¹/₁₆	7⅞	5¾

Typical stem cross section showing the locations of A, B, D, and E

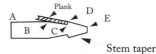

Stem taper

Definitions and Abbreviations
WL = Waterline
FP = Forward perpendicular
A = Inner line of stem
B = Bearding line
C = Inner rabbet or ghost line
D = Rabbet
E = Stem face

Backbone (see Figure 2)

Stem (includes material for forefoot, stem knee, transom knee, deadwood, sternpost, mast-step)—Honduras mahogany, fir, or white oak; one piece 1⅜ inches by 8 inches, 8 feet long.

Keel—Honduras mahogany, fir, or white oak; one piece 1⅜ inches by 1½ inches, 13 feet long.

Keel batten—white oak, one piece ⅝ inch by 2½ inches, 13 feet long.

Transom—Honduras mahogany or fir, one piece ¹³/₁₆ inch by 7 inches, 9 feet long; one roll plastic wrapping tape.

Daggerboard case—Honduras mahogany or fir, one piece ¾ inch by ⅝ inch, 4 feet long; ¼-inch (6-millimeter) mahogany marine plywood, 1 foot by 2 feet.

Drafting equipment (for more detailed description, see "Materials list" in Chapter II)

Table (made of two hollow-core doors and three saw horses).

Drafting vellum or Mylar, 30 inches by 9 feet.

Pencils, white rubber erasers.

Drafting batten (or spline), ¼ inch by ⅜ inch by 5 feet polycarbonate (Lexan), or adjustable splines.

Rulers—4-foot aluminum; steel carpenter's square; 18-to-24-inch steel ruler.

Drafting dots (masking tape used to anchor the drafting film).

Light-gauge finish nails, ½ pound.

Awl, push-pins, light-gauge nail.

Ball of string.

Your workspace

Each step of this project levies different requirements upon your shop. I cut out all of the parts for the setup before I build the jig; this gives me all the workspace in the shop to move long boards around. I develop the parts of the setup on a temporary table made up of two hollow-core doors set up on three saw horses. Screw the doors to the saw horses with 2½-inch drywall screws so things don't move around. When you are finished with the table, you can quickly dismantle it and store it away until you need it again. One door can be set up as a layout table for the interior parts if you need it.

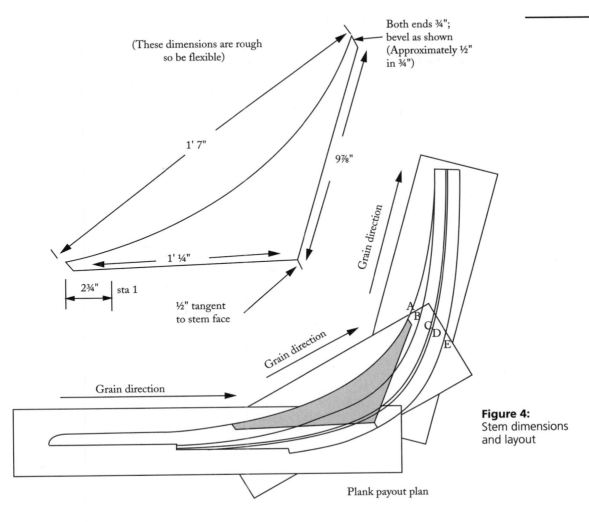

(These dimensions are rough so be flexible)

Both ends ¾"; bevel as shown (Approximately ½" in ¾")

1' 7"

9⅞"

Grain direction

1' ¼"

2¾"   sta 1

½" tangent to stem face

Grain direction

Grain direction

A
B
C
D
E

Figure 4:
Stem dimensions and layout

Plank payout plan

Step A: Draft and build the stem assembly (Figures 3–7)

In this section you will draft the stem assembly, cut out and fit the parts, bed and fasten the assembly, and cut the rabbet.

1. Spread out the vellum on the table, aligning the bottom edge to the table edge, and secure it with the drafting dots. You are going to draw the profile of the stem assembly full size. You will first draw the grid (see Figure 3).

2. From the left-hand side of the vellum, measure out 1 inch. Draw a perpendicular line here. Moving to the right from this line, draw perpendiculars and mark them at 9½ inches (Station 1A), 1 foot 7 inches (Station 1), and 3 feet 1 inch (FP— forward perpendicular; see Figure 3). Draw a horizontal baseline 1 inch up from the edge of the table. Draw the horizontals at 6, 9, 12, 15, 18, 21, 27 (sheerline), and 29 (jig line) inches. Draw a diagonal line from the intersection of WL (water-line) 15 inches to a point on the baseline 9 inches to the right of Station 1.

3. From the table of offsets, measure out from the baseline and mark the points on the diagonal. Then working left from the FP, mark the points on the waterlines. Drive light finish nails into the points one line at a time and spring your drafting batten around them. Outline the stem, lines B, C, D, and the forward end of the keel and keel batten. This last will ensure that your stem assembly will fit to the keel assembly when the time comes.

4. Draw the parts of the stem assembly (see Figure 4), beginning with the stem knee. Starting 2¾ inches to the left of Station 1 on line A, draw the profile of the stem knee.

5. Put the stem stock under the vellum. Line up each part of the stem assembly so that the grain is lengthwise along the part. Arrange the parts so that you maximize the use of the stock. With an awl or nail, push through the Mylar into the stock along the outside profile of each stem part to make a series of holes. Using nails and your batten to spring a line through the holes, mark the lines. Use a ruler to mark the straight lines. Do not mark lines B, C, and D now; it is better to mark these lines after the parts are fitted and joined.

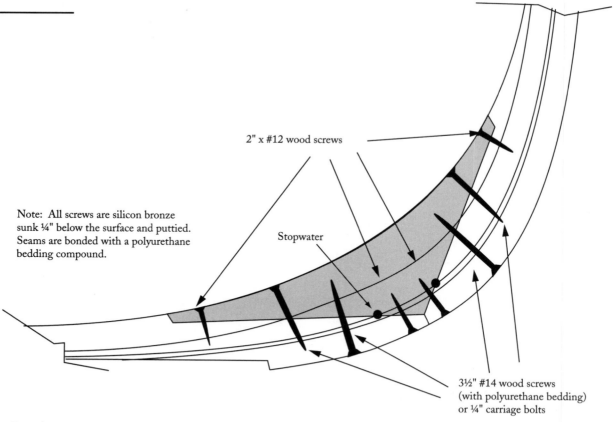

2" x #12 wood screws

Note: All screws are silicon bronze
sunk ¼" below the surface and puttied.
Seams are bonded with a polyurethane
bedding compound.

Stopwater

3½" #14 wood screws
(with polyurethane bedding)
or ¼" carriage bolts

Figure 5:
Stem construction plan

6. Cut out the stem knee, forefoot, and stem on the bandsaw. To minimize fitting time, cut carefully, leaving only the line. Use your block plane to fit the parts. Using 2-inch #12 bronze screws at the ends, fasten the parts together (see Figure 5).

7. Define the shape of the stem taper between lines D and E (see Figure 6). Set your combination square to ⁵⁄₁₆ inch and use it to mark a line ⁵⁄₁₆ inch from each edge of the forward face of the stem (see the cross-section in Figure 1). This will line out the ¾-inch stem face.

8. The traditional method: Mark where the stopwaters will go. There will be two ⁵⁄₁₆-inch stopwaters made out of softwood, usually cedar. Whittle the stopwater stock to rough shape and drive through a ⁵⁄₁₆-inch hole drilled in a steel plate (sometimes this hole needs to be ⁹⁄₃₂ inch). The stopwaters are installed where the stem knee crosses line C (the apex line). With your pencil, mark where the stopwaters will go so that you will not put a bolt through the stopwaters. Then lay out for two ¼-inch carriage bolts through each arm of the stem knee. From the center of the stem face, drill ¼-inch holes for the bolts. The head of a ¼-inch carriage bolt is approximately ⅝ inch, which takes up most of the stem face and could

cause a breakout on the side of the stem. To avoid this I grind off two sides of the head, leaving a rectangular shape. Then I cut the ⅜-inch countersink with a ¼-inch chisel. Lay the bolts alongside the stem assembly to make sure that at least ⅜ inch protrudes through the inside of the stem assembly. If it is longer than that, you can always cut some off after the assembly is complete. When all looks good, unscrew the assembly, bed the joints, and refasten with the screws and bolts. Then drill for the stopwaters. Make sure that the stopwaters are drilled at the intersection of the stem knee and line C. The hole must not reach outside line D. If necessary, it can be slightly more toward line B. We want it to be under the plank. The stopwaters should be a drive-fit.

Polyurethane-bedding method: With this construction method there is no requirement for stopwaters, as the joint will be watertight. You can use bolts or 3-inch #14 bronze screws. If you use screws, make sure that they cross the line of the joint at an angle. Pre-drill with a countersink and install the screws or bolts. When all fits, disassemble and reassemble with polyurethane bedding compound in the joints. Wear gloves and a respirator. Clean up immediately with stove alcohol (the safest) or lacquer thinner. Good ventilation is a must.

a. With a chisel, cut at C straight down ⁵⁄₁₆" (solid line). Take small cuts at at a time (⅛").
b. As you work down the stem, clean it out to D and B.
c. Check it regularly with a piece of plank scrap.
d. To shape the stem, plane off the corner from D to E leaving a ¾" flat on the stem.

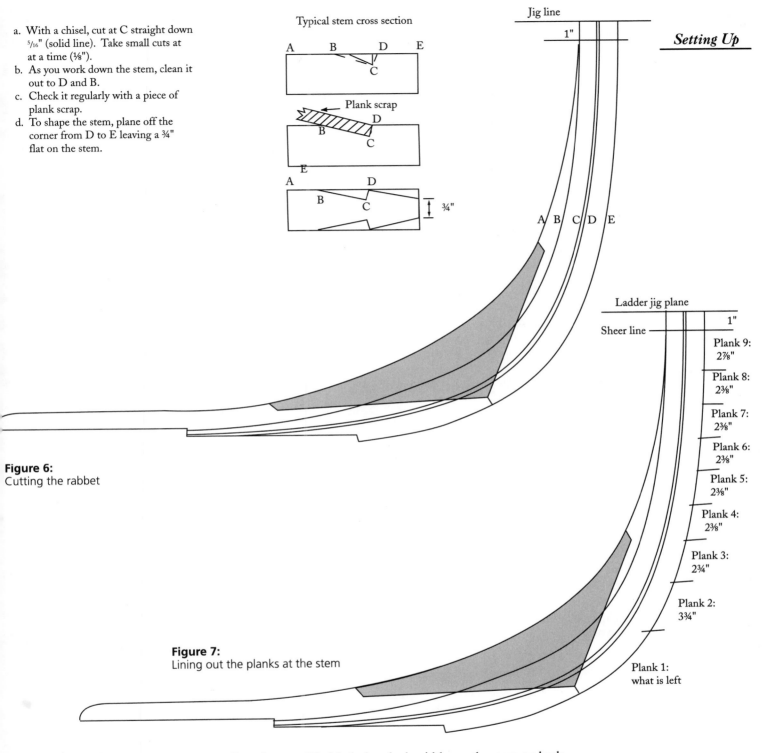

Typical stem cross section

Plank scrap

Jig line

1"

A B C D E

Ladder jig plane

Sheer line

1"

Plank 9: 2⅞"

Plank 8: 2⅜"

Plank 7: 2⅜"

Plank 6: 2⅜"

Plank 5: 2⅜"

Plank 4: 2⅜"

Plank 3: 2¾"

Plank 2: 3¾"

Plank 1: what is left

Figure 6:
Cutting the rabbet

Figure 7:
Lining out the planks at the stem

9. Cut the rabbet by overlaying the vellum drawing over the stock and punching through along the lines with an awl or push pins. On both sides of the stem assembly, mark and draw lines B, C, and D. Chisel straight down at C, ⁵⁄₁₆ inch (see Figure 6). Then chisel across from B to C, and from D to C. Work carefully and slowly. When the rabbet is roughed out, use your 3-inch trim plane to clean up and fair out the rabbet where you can. For the rest, use a chisel. After the setup is complete, you will check your work with battens simulating the planks and clean up the rabbet some more.

10. Mark the plank widths on the stem on both sides (see Figure 7). Then set the stem assembly aside.

a. Follow directions in step 1 and mark mold shapes for stations 1–7 and the transom.

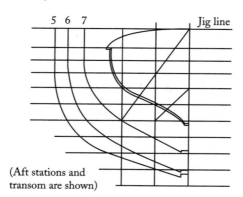

(Aft stations and transom are shown)

b. Lay the drawing over the plank and push through with an awl at approximately 1" intervals to outline the mold shape. Spring batten through the points and mark.

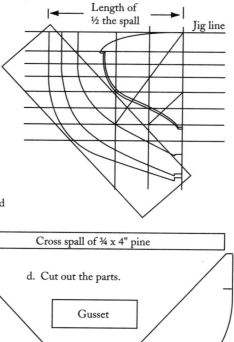

c. ¾" x 11" pine plank with mold outline. Screw two planks together and cut with the bandsaw.

Mark the sheer on all molds.

Cross spall of ¾ x 4" pine

d. Cut out the parts.

Gusset

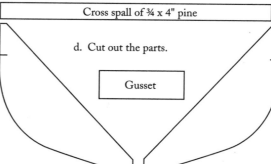

Centerline

e. Screw and glue.

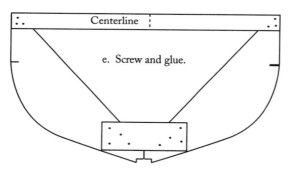

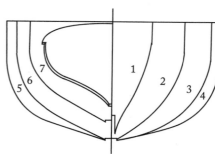

Body plan showing stations and transom; molds will be made for each station.

Figure 8:
Building the molds

Step B: Build the molds
(Figures 8–15, Figure 19)
In this section you will draft the mold shapes, cut out the parts for the molds, and assemble them (see Figure 8).

1. Measuring 1 inch from the right-hand edge of the Mylar (or vellum) and moving to the left, draw a perpendicular for the centerline of Molds 5 through 7. Draw another perpendicular for the centerline for Molds 1 through 4 from the left-hand edge.

2. Draw the grid. First draw the horizontal waterlines, as shown in Figure 9; then draw the vertical buttock lines. Mark the points and draw the outline of Mold 5 as shown; be sure to mark the location of the sheer. Continue to mark and draw Molds 6 and 7 as shown on Figures 10 and 11.

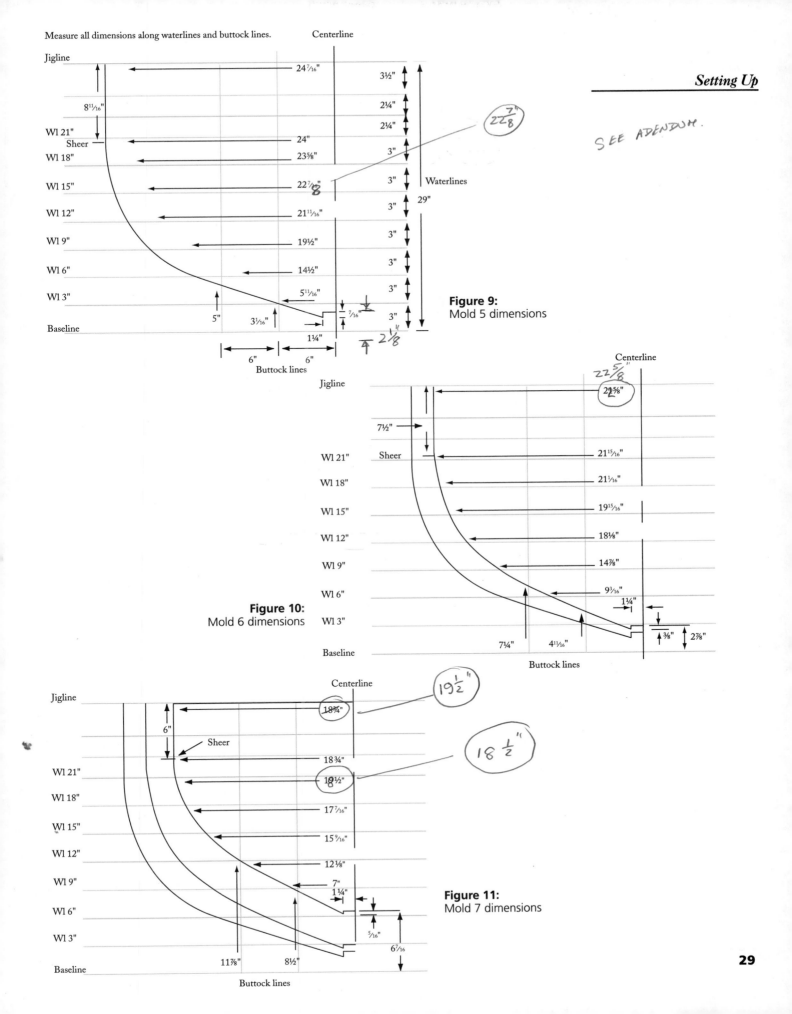

Measure all dimensions along waterlines and buttock lines.

SEE ADENDUM.

Figure 9:
Mold 5 dimensions

Figure 10:
Mold 6 dimensions

Figure 11:
Mold 7 dimensions

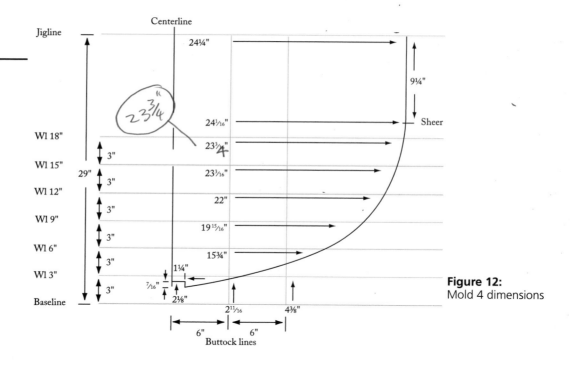

Centerline

Jigline

24¼"

9¼"

24¹⁄₁₆" Sheer

23⅞"

Wl 18" 3"

29" 23³⁄₁₆"

Wl 15" 3"

Wl 12" 3" 22"

Wl 9" 3" 19¹⁵⁄₁₆"

Wl 6" 3" 15¾"

Wl 3" 3" 1¼"

Baseline ⁷⁄₁₆" 2⅛"

2¹¹⁄₁₆" 4⅜"

6" 6"

Buttock lines

Figure 12:
Mold 4 dimensions

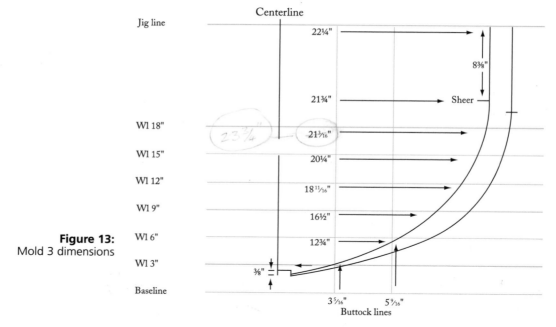

Centerline

Jig line

22¼"

8⅜"

21¾" Sheer

Wl 18"

21³⁄₁₆"

Wl 15"

20¼"

Wl 12"

18¹¹⁄₁₆"

Wl 9"

16½"

Figure 13: Wl 6" 12¾"
Mold 3 dimensions

Wl 3" ⅜"

Baseline

3⁵⁄₁₆" 5⁹⁄₁₆"

Buttock lines

3. Draw the grid for the molds at Stations 1–4 (see Figures 12–15). Mark the points and draw the mold shapes as before.

4. Now you will build the molds. Study Figure 8 carefully. You will start by sliding 1- by 12-inch (¹³⁄₁₆ inch by 11½ inches, actual dimensions) pine shelving under the vellum, as shown in Figure 8 at Mold 5. Using an awl, a fine nail, or a push-pin, push through the Mylar into the pine and outline the mold half. Using your batten and a ruler, draw the outline of half of the mold. Cut out the mold half and check it against the drawing. It should be as close as you can get it. Be especially careful that the cutout for the keel batten is accurate. This will be important when you fit the keel assembly to the molds. When you are satisfied, use it as a pattern to make an identical second half. Check this carefully also.

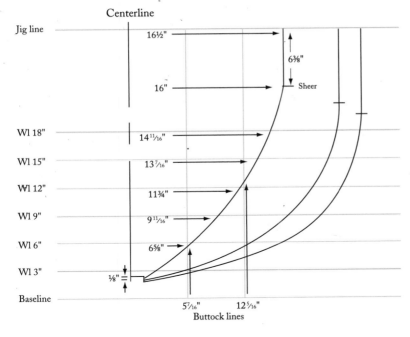

Figure 14:
Mold 2 dimensions

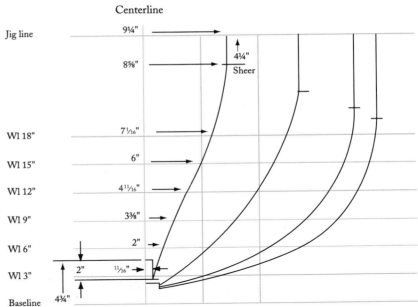

Figure 15:
Mold 1 dimensions

5. Now you will make the cross spall out of 1 x 4-inch (¾ inch by 3½ inches) shelving pine. Measure out two times the distance along the jig line at the top of Figure 8. Cut the spall. Draw a line at the center of the spall; this will help aligning the molds when you set up.

6. Line up the mold halves using the edge of the table and place the spall over the ends. The top edges of the molds should line up perfectly. If they don't, check everything against your drawing; mistakes happen all the time. If everything fits, use a piece of scrap pine to fashion a gusset to join the two halves of the mold.

7. Clamp the ends of the molds and cross spall to the table so they won't jump around, and fasten with 1¼-inch drywall screws. Do the same for the gusset.

8. Repeat the process for Molds 6, 7, and 1 through 4. Be sure to check your work. When you are done, put the molds aside.

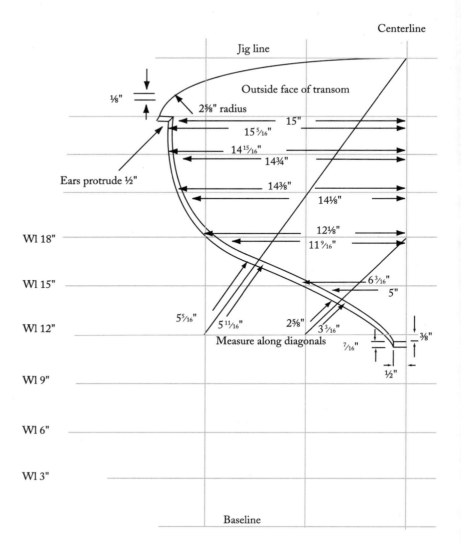

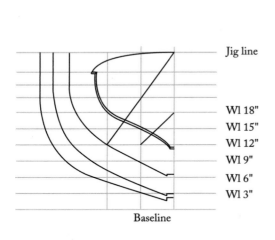

Figure 16:
Transom dimensions

Step C: Shape the transom
(Figures 16–19)

1. Using the vellum you used for Molds 4–7, draw the transom's inside and outside dimensions (see Figure 16).

2. The transom can be made up of any number of planks (see Figure 17). I show three planks gotten out of 7-inch-wide stock; if your stock allows two or four, that is no problem. I show 36-inch widths to allow for any damage caused by clamps, but you can be more efficient with the stock if you think the problem out. I use the leftover scrap for knees. Plane the edges carefully to maintain a square edge. You can clamp a 6-inch-long piece of wood to the bottom of the plane to act as a guide to hold the plane square to the plank. Check the fit of the planks carefully.

3. The planks can be edge-glued with epoxy. If you edge-glue, put clamps at the seams to keep them from misaligning when you clamp them up. I prefer to spline the joints (see Figure 17), using a router and a ¼-inch butterfly bit. For a spline, plywood is best; plain-sawn planking is next in preference. The splines will be about ¼ inch by 1 inch. Check the fit before you glue. If you have a biscuit joiner, you can use that also.

4. Use three or four pipe clamps to glue the planks together. Alternate the clamps on each side to even up the pressure. As you start to apply pressure, the assembly will tend to bow in one direction. Check for this with a straightedge. Before you apply full pressure, clamp a straight 2 by 4 to the bowed side; this will straighten things up. The surface of the 2 by 4 should be protected from the glue with plastic wrapping tape. Wipe off as much glue as you can. Wear gloves and use a respirator in poorly ventilated spaces.

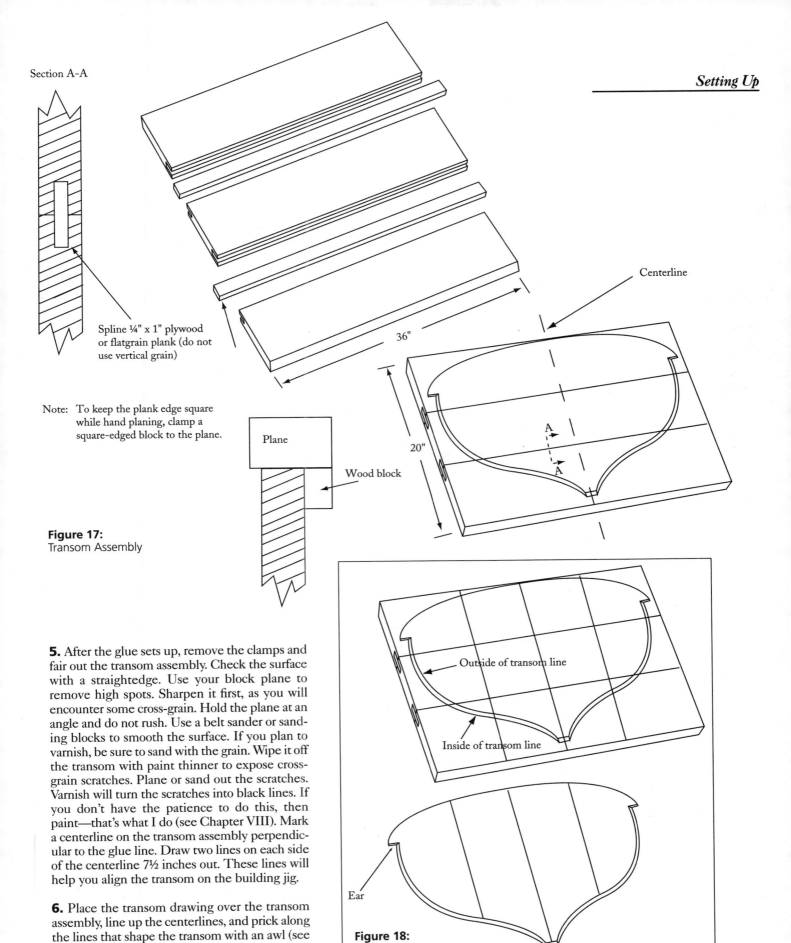

Section A-A

Spline ¼" x 1" plywood
or flatgrain plank (do not
use vertical grain)

Note: To keep the plank edge square
while hand planing, clamp a
square-edged block to the plane.

Plane

Wood block

Figure 17:
Transom Assembly

Centerline

36"

20"

A

A

5. After the glue sets up, remove the clamps and fair out the transom assembly. Check the surface with a straightedge. Use your block plane to remove high spots. Sharpen it first, as you will encounter some cross-grain. Hold the plane at an angle and do not rush. Use a belt sander or sanding blocks to smooth the surface. If you plan to varnish, be sure to sand with the grain. Wipe it off the transom with paint thinner to expose cross-grain scratches. Plane or sand out the scratches. Varnish will turn the scratches into black lines. If you don't have the patience to do this, then paint—that's what I do (see Chapter VIII). Mark a centerline on the transom assembly perpendicular to the glue line. Draw two lines on each side of the centerline 7½ inches out. These lines will help you align the transom on the building jig.

6. Place the transom drawing over the transom assembly, line up the centerlines, and prick along the lines that shape the transom with an awl (see Figure 18). Spring a batten through the points and mark the lines.

Outside of transom line

Inside of transom line

Ear

Figure 18:
Shape the transom

Foot

33

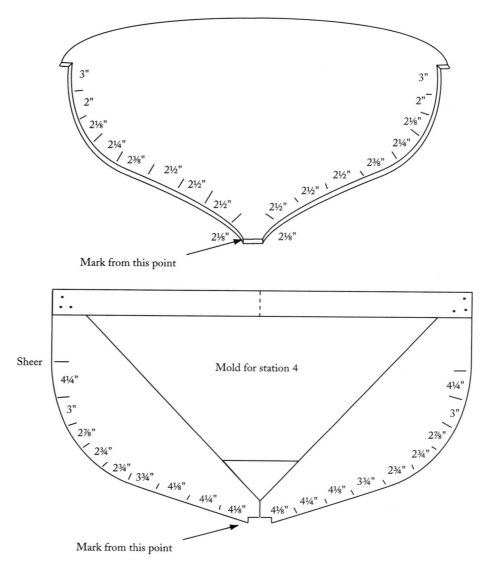

Figure 19:
Plank lines for the transom and Mold 4

7. Cut the transom out on the bandsaw, cutting to the outside lines (this is the shape of the inside of the transom). With your spokeshave, plane from the inside line to the outside line. Use a dovetail saw or fine-toothed Japanese saw to cut the lines at the ears.

8. Mark the plank lines on the transom and Mold 4 (see Figure 19). These marks represent the top edges of the planks. Put the transom aside.

Step D: Cut out and assemble the backbone (Figures 20–26)
The backbone assembly is made up of the keel, keel batten, deadwood, transom knee, and sternpost. Be especially careful that you check all measurements. The length is critical to the setup. Be sure to pre-drill and countersink for all fastenings.

1. On your sheet of vellum, draw the deadwood and transom knee (see Figure 20). The angle of the transom knee should complement the angle of the deadwood. In other words, when the knee is placed on top of the deadwood, a straight edge will be created. This is important, as the knee sets up the transom.

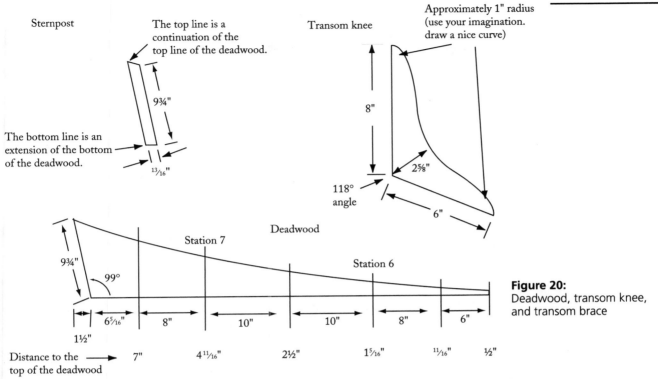

Sternpost

The top line is a continuation of the top line of the deadwood.

9¾"

The bottom line is an extension of the bottom of the deadwood.

¹³⁄₁₆"

Transom knee

Approximately 1" radius (use your imagination. draw a nice curve)

8"

2⅝"

118° angle

6"

Deadwood

Station 7

Station 6

9¾"

99°

6⁵⁄₁₆"   8"   10"   10"   8"   6"

1½"

Distance to the top of the deadwood   7"   4¹¹⁄₁₆"   2½"   1⁵⁄₁₆"   ¹¹⁄₁₆"   ½"

Figure 20:
Deadwood, transom knee, and transom brace

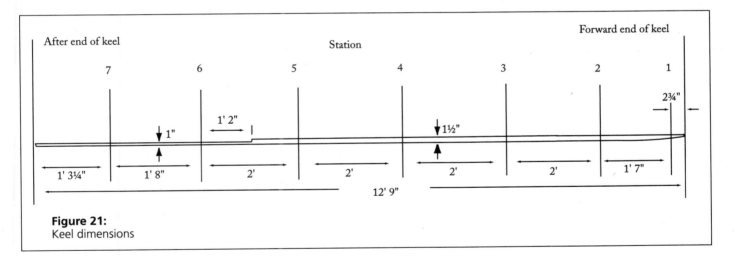

After end of keel

Station

Forward end of keel

7   6   5   4   3   2   1

2¾"

1' 2"

1"   1½"

1' 3¼"   1' 8"   2'   2'   2'   2'   1' 7"

12' 9"

Figure 21:
Keel dimensions

2. Now lay the vellum on the 1⅜-inch stock, and mark the deadwood and the transom knee. Cut out these parts, leaving the line, and clean up to the line with a spokeshave and block plane.

3. Measure the sternpost and cut it out (Figure 20). The sternpost is a cap on the end of the deadwood, so it should fit as an extension of the deadwood.

4. Now cut out the keel (Figure 21). Mark the station lines on both sides of the keel stock. Check the shape of the forward end on the stem drawing to make sure the stem will fit. The deadwood and the sternpost will fit into the ½-inch cut in the after end of the keel.

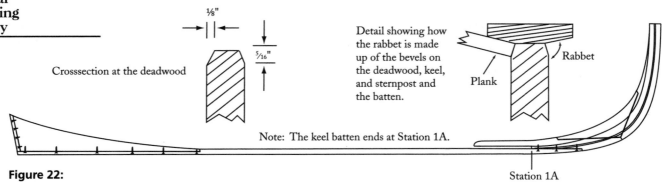

1/8"

5/16"

Crosssection at the deadwood

Detail showing how
the rabbet is made
up of the bevels on
the deadwood, keel,
and sternpost and
the batten.

Rabbet

Plank

Note: The keel batten ends at Station 1A.

Station 1A

Figure 22:
Assembling the stem, keel, deadwood, and sternpost and cutting the rabbet

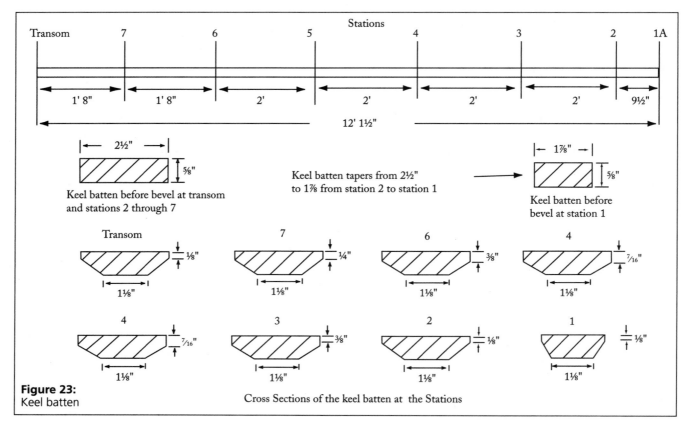

Figure 23:
Keel batten

Cross Sections of the keel batten at the Stations

5. Fasten the deadwood and keel with 2-inch #12 screws spaced 4 inches where you can and shorter #8 screws at the forward end of the deadwood (see Figure 22). If the screws break through the top of the deadwood, file them off after the final fitting. Fasten the sternpost with 1½-inch #8 screws spaced 4 inches apart. Do not use adhesives yet.

6. Fit the stem assembly to the forward end of the keel. There will be a gap left for the keel batten (see Figure 22). Fasten the keel to the stem with #12 screws. Note where the rabbet (line D) and apex line (line C) on the stem strike the keel (see Figures 3 and 6). Fair the apex line on the stem to the top of the keel and the stem rabbet line to the rabbet line on the keel. Note that the lines come off the stem before the end of the keel. It is important that the rabbet be a continuous curve along the stem, keel, deadwood, and sternpost. The lines should fair in about Station 1A.

7. Now fair the stem taper (from line D to E) into the keel. The stem taper disappears from the beginning of the keel to somewhere between Stations 1A and 2. Use a fairing batten to line out the transition lines on the bottom of the keel. (A fairing batten is a long, thin piece of wood, possibly one of the battens you will make to fair the molds and line out the planking; see Step H, "Check the rabbet and transom bevels.") Eyeball this line carefully. Go ahead and plane the transition.

8. The keel batten is white oak finished 2½ inches by ⅝ inch. It is best if it is plain-sawn, as it has to take a bend over the deadwood. Take a short piece of scrap from the batten stock, and slide it under the stem to make sure it will fit between the keel and the stem.

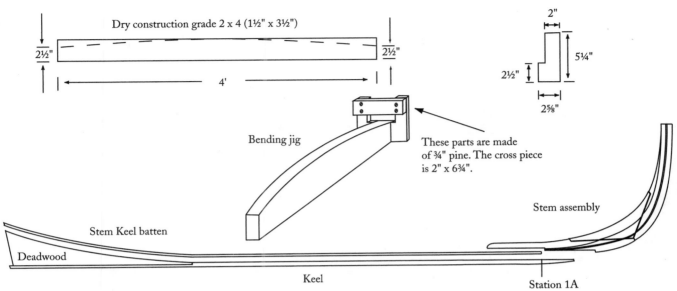

Figure 24:
Fitting the keel batten

9. Cut the length of the stock to 12 feet 1½ inches and mark the stations. On the bottom of the stock, set your combination square to ¹³⁄₁₆ inch and mark a line on each side. This should leave a 1⅛-inch space down the center of the batten. The keel batten tapers from 2½ inches to 1⅞ inches from Station 2 to Station 1A (see Figures 23 and 24). Use a batten to spring a fair curve on each side; then cut the taper.

10. At each station measure down from the top of the keel batten on each side the distance shown in Figure 23. Then spring a fairing batten through the points. Clamp the fairing batten onto the side of the keel batten at each point and draw a line. Then plane off the corner on each side of the keel batten (Figures 23 and 24).

11. Push the forward end of the keel batten under the stem to check the fit and to check how the bearding line, apex line, and rabbet line fair into the keel and stem. Do not try to force the batten into the bend over the deadwood; you will pre-bend this later. Remove the batten and make adjustments to the forward end as required. Repeat this process until you are satisfied. When the keel batten is inserted, mark the general area where it bends over the deadwood.

12. Remove the keel batten and mark the rabbet at the deadwood and keel. With your combination square set to ⁵⁄₁₆ inch, mark a line along both sides of the top of the sternpost, deadwood, and keel assembly and another ⅛ inch from each side of the top (see the detail of the cross-section at the deadwood in Figure 22). Fair these lines into the stem rabbet. Plane off the corner of the backbone assembly from the sternpost to the stem.

13. Now remove the sternpost from the assembly. Build the bending jig as shown in Figure 24. Place plastic sheeting, then a terrycloth towel over the jig. Place the after end of the keel batten into the jig and wrap the toweling around the batten. Apply pressure until there is no spring in the plank. Pour hot (boiling or near boiling) water over the toweling, soaking it thoroughly. (The water can be boiled on a stove, heated in a coffee maker, or can even be very hot tap water.) Wrap the plastic around the toweling and let it sit for five minutes. Start to increase the clamping pressure until the easy spring is taken up. Open the plastic and pour on more hot water. Keep repeating this process until the plank bends to the jig. It should take 15 to 20 minutes. Clamp the batten to the jig and let it sit overnight.

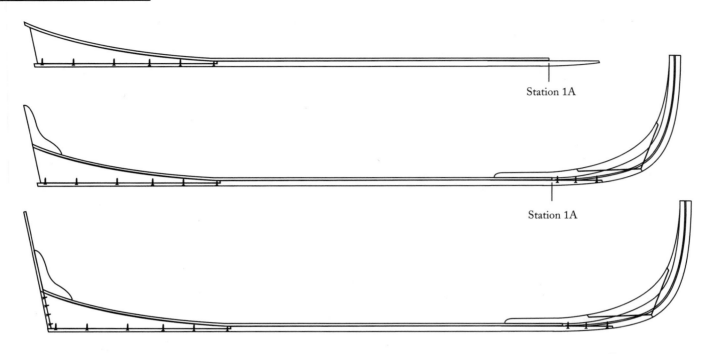

Station 1A

Station 1A

Figure 25:
Assemble the
backbone

14. Take the batten from the jig and slide it under the stem. Work the batten into the curve of the deadwood. Make sure that the 1⅛-inch surface at the bottom of the batten matches the 1⅛-inch surface at the top of the backbone assembly. Clamp this assembly to one of the straight 2-by-4s you bought for the ladder jig to ensure that the bottom of the keel is straight and not curved. Check the assembly. Screw every 6 inches along the batten into the backbone with 1½-inch #8 screws (see Figure 25). Screw through the stem into the batten and up into the batten through the keel with #12 screws. Traditionalists would put two ¼-inch carriage bolts here and bed with oil-based bedding compound, but the bolts are not necessary if you use polyurethane bedding compound.

15. Check the backbone assembly thoroughly for alignment, fit, and that the rabbet is fair. Then disassemble, bed, and reassemble (see Figure 25). Traditionalists then install stopwaters at the intersection of the stem and keel and at both ends of the deadwood at the apex line; this is not necessary if you are using polyurethane bedding compound. Clamp the assembly to a straight, stiff surface like the edge of a 2 x 4 until the compound has cured; then remove the 2 by 4 and clamps.

16. Using the after face of the deadwood as a guide, use your fine Japanese pull saw to cut off the keel batten flush with the after end of the deadwood.

17. Fit the transom knee to the top of the keel batten. The 8-inch arm of the knee should be flush with the deadwood and the keel batten (see Figure 25). You should be able to align a straight-edge along the end of the deadwood, keel batten, and the after face of the transom knee. When it looks good, remove, bed, and fasten with #12 screws. You can screw down and up through the after face of the deadwood.

18. Bed and fasten the sternpost with 1½-inch #8 screws. You should have already fitted this.

19. On both sides of the keel and deadwood, mark the station lines and continue them up and over the keel batten. Do not measure for the station lines along the batten, as the distance between stations along the batten are longer due to the bend. Measure up from the keel.

20. Mark centerlines at the top of the transom knee and the sternpost. Then mark centerlines on the inside and outside face of the transom. On the inside and outside faces of the transom, mark two parallel lines 7½ inches on each side of the centerline.

21. Set the backbone assembly upright and clamp it there; the Black & Decker Workmate bench is great for stuff like this. Then fit the transom to the backbone, using the centerlines to align it. Clamp it up. On the inside, mark where the top of the transom knee strikes the transom. Take off the clamps and drill three holes along the centerline of the transom under the knee. Reclamp and drill and countersink for #8 1½-inch screws. Install the screws.

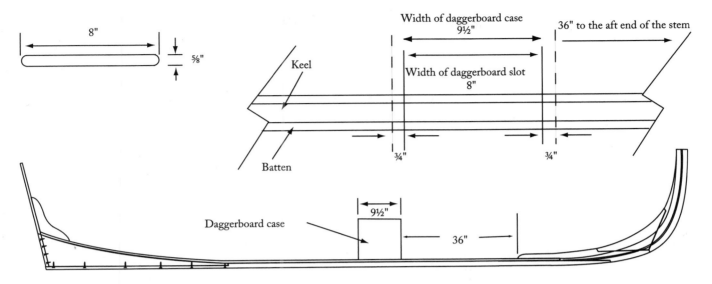

Figure 26:
The daggerboard slot

22. Remove the transom and set it aside.

23. If you are going to sail this boat, you will have to install a daggerboard (see Figure 26). Now is the best time to cut the slot. First, review Figures 26 and 27 carefully. The length of the daggerboard case is 9½ inches and the slot is 8 inches, starting 36¾ inches from the after end of the stem. Mark a line across the batten at this point and another 8 inches farther aft. You will drill a ⅝-inch hole at each end of the slot, using a ⅝-inch bit. Draw a centerline between the two lines and mark a drill center ⅙ inch from each end. If you have a drill press, you can make a drilling jig by drilling a ⅙-inch hole into a piece of oak. Then align the jig over the center mark and drill through the batten and keel. It may not go all the way through, but this will give you a pilot hole square to the batten. If your batten is not quite square to the keel or if you are not certain, locate the center mark of the hole on both the batten and the bottom of the keel and drill from both sides. You can do this by marking around the keel and batten with a combination square. Hopefully they will meet in the middle; if not, you can make an adjustment with a file and a chisel later. Then drill with the ⅝-inch paddle bit (also known as an Irwin Speedbor bit) from both sides.

24. Cut the rest of the slot with a circular saw, as shown in Figure 26. Finish the slot with a handsaw. In a pinch, a jigsaw will cut the slot. It is hard to cut a clean, straight line with a jigsaw, so you may have to clean up with a file and chisel. If you have to use the jigsaw, use a metal cutting blade; this leaves a smooth cut. Square off the ends of the slot with your chisel. Score the square ends with your chisel first, to keep the outside of the cut clean. Take small cuts with the chisel, working from both top and bottom toward the middle.

25. Bed and fasten the transom to the backbone.

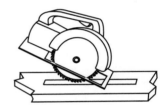

Note: Circular saw technique:
a. Start at an angle
b. Push forward as you drop
c. Never pull back
d. Finish off with a handsaw

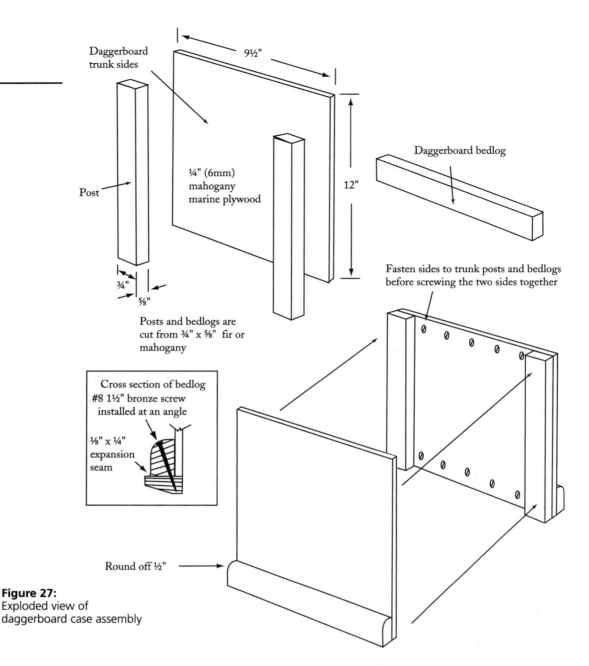

Daggerboard
trunk sides

9½"

Post

¼" (6mm)
mahogany
marine plywood

12"

¾"

⅝"

Posts and bedlogs are
cut from ¾" x ⅝" fir or
mahogany

Daggerboard bedlog

Fasten sides to trunk posts and bedlogs
before screwing the two sides together

Cross section of bedlog
#8 1½" bronze screw
installed at an angle

⅛" x ¼"
expansion
seam

Round off ½"

Figure 27:
Exploded view of
daggerboard case assembly

Step E: Build the daggerboard case
(Figures 26–27)

The daggerboard case is made at this time. It will be assembled and fitted then set aside to be finished later (see Figure 27).

1. Cut two pieces of ¼-inch mahogany marine plywood 12 inches by 9½ inches. Much of this plywood is manufactured overseas and is sold as 6 millimeter (6mm) thick. The bedlogs and posts are cut from ⅝-inch-by-¾-inch stock. Cut the two posts at 12 inches and the two bedlogs at 9½ inches. With a router or block plane, round off one corner of the bedlog with a ½-inch radius.

2. Fasten the posts to one side of the case with ¾-inch #8 screws. Fasten through the plywood into the posts. Then fasten a bedlog to this assembly, screwing through the plywood.

3. Fasten the second bedlog to the remaining side. Then fasten this side to the other side. Screw through the plywood into the post.

4. At each end of the bedlog, install a 2-inch #8 bronze screw through the assembly.

5. Unscrew the assembly, bed the parts in epoxy glue or polyurethane compound, and refasten the case. Clean up thoroughly and immediately.

6. Cut a ⅛-inch-by-¼-inch expansion seam around the bottom edge of the bedlogs. Then sand the case, rounding the corners 1/16 inch, and fit the case over the slot, fastening it with 1½-inch #8 bronze screws. Then reinstall it, bedding with polyurethane compound. This is not a traditional construction plan for a daggerboard case, so traditionalists should use polyurethane bedding here, too. Sorry, but it's just simpler and lighter construction.

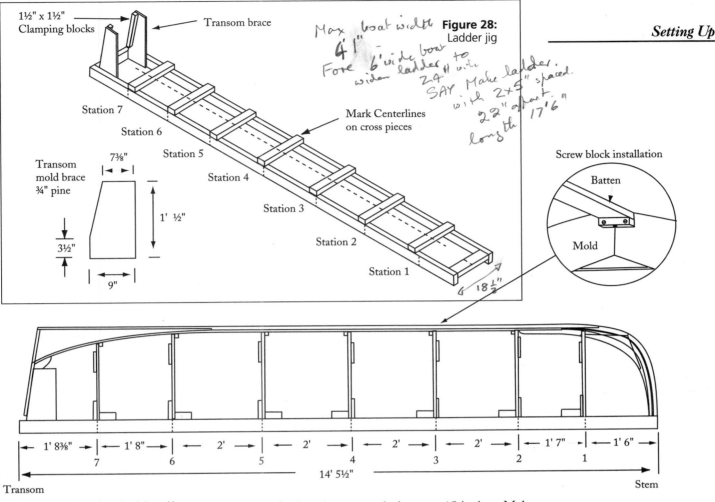

Figure 28:
Ladder jig

Handwritten notes:
Max boat width 4' 1"
Fore 6' wide boat widen ladder to 24" with SAY Make ladder with 2×5" spaced. 22" apart. length 17'6"

1½" x 1½" Clamping blocks

Transom brace

Station 7

Station 6

Transom mold brace ¾" pine

7⅜"

1' ½"

3½"

9"

Station 5

Station 4

Mark Centerlines on cross pieces

Station 3

Station 2

Station 1

18½"

Screw block installation

Batten

Mold

← 1' 8⅜" → ← 1' 8" → ← 2' → ← 2' → ← 2' → ← 2' → ← 1' 7" → ← 1' 6" →
7   6   5   4   3   2   1

14' 5½"

Transom

Stem

Figure 29:
The setup

Step F: Build the ladder jig (Figure 28)
The ladder jig is the foundation of the setup. It must be stiff, straight, have no twist, and have structural integrity so that you can move it around without losing the shape of the boat. Study Figures 28 and 29 carefully.

1. Check the long 2 by 4s (actual dimension 1½ inches by 3½ inches) for straightness, and cut them to 14 feet 5½ inches. Set these pieces side-by-side on two saw horses. To make sure that there is no twist in the jig, use a piece of string to make sure the jig fits into one plane. To do this, clamp the 2 by 4s to the saw horses, edges up, and tack finish nails at both ends of each piece. Wrap the string around the nails at the after of the jig and bring the ends of the string down to the forward end of the jig. Cross the string (thus forming an X) and touch the ends to the forward corners of the jig. If the jig is in one plane, the string will just barely touch at the center. If there is a twist, it will either show a gap or one section will bend over the other at the center. If your test shows a twist, loosen the clamps under the low corner and use a wedge to adjust the height until the string just touches at the center.

2. Cut the two end-pieces to 15 inches. Make sure the ends of these pieces are perfectly square; this is the key to a good setup. Fasten the end-pieces between the long pieces with 2½-inch drywall screws. The after end-piece is vertical, and the forward piece is horizontal.

3. Mark the stations as shown in Figure 29. Check the stations for square with your carpenter's square across the jig. Cut out seven cross-pieces 18 inches long. The cross-piece at Station 1 is placed two thicknesses of your mold material (two times ¹³⁄₁₆ inch or whatever the actual thickness is) on the after side of the Station 1 mark.

4. The cross-pieces at Stations 2, 3, and 4 are installed on the after side of the station mark, and the cross-pieces at Stations 5, 6, and 7 are placed on the forward side. Fasten the cross-pieces with 2½-inch screws.

5. Cut out two transom braces out of shelving pine (see Figure 28). Install them at the after end of the jig. The bottom of the braces fit into the aft corners of the jig, are even with the bottom of the side pieces, and are installed with 1¼-inch drywall screws.

6. Draw a centerline on the end-pieces and cross-pieces. Check with your string to ensure that they line up down the length of the jig.

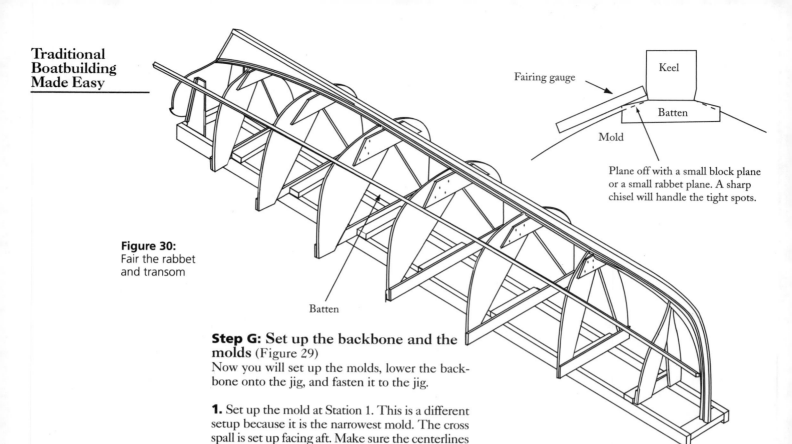

Keel

Fairing gauge

Batten

Mold

Plane off with a small block plane
or a small rabbet plane. A sharp
chisel will handle the tight spots.

Figure 30:
Fair the rabbet
and transom

Batten

Step G: Set up the backbone and the
molds (Figure 29)
Now you will set up the molds, lower the backbone onto the jig, and fasten it to the jig.

1. Set up the mold at Station 1. This is a different
setup because it is the narrowest mold. The cross
spall is set up facing aft. Make sure the centerlines
match, then fasten the mold to the cross-piece.

2. Set up and fasten the rest of the molds. The jig
is designed so that when the molds are set up, the
forward faces of the forward molds and Station 4
will be on the station marks, and the after faces
of the after molds will be on the station marks (see
Figure 29). The molds should align with the centerline and the station marks. When everything is
aligned, fasten the molds in place.

3. Place the backbone over the molds. The stem
should touch the forward end of the jig and be lined
up with the centerline. Fasten it to the jig by toe-
nailing it to the horizontal end brace with a 2½-inch
drywall screw. If all your measurements are correct,
the transom should lie on the transom braces. The
keel batten should fit into the batten pockets cut
into the molds. If your pocket is too deep, you can
wedge the batten up. The keel should be straight;
eyeball it carefully. Line up the molds with the station lines on the keel batten. If the stations are
marked correctly, when the marks on the batten are
aligned with molds, the molds should be perpendicular to the jig. Do not panic if there are slight dif-
ferences, but do not hesitate to check your
measurements. Mistakes are a chronic problem in
boatbuilding, so never hesitate to check your work.

4. Mold 1 can be fastened directly to the end of
the stem. The other stations require a screw block
(see Figure 29). This can be a piece of pine ¹³⁄₁₆
inch by 1 inch by 2⅝ inches. Over the deadwood,
you will have to bevel the screw block to fit the
keel batten. Pre-drill the blocks for two screws
into the mold and one into the batten, then fasten the blocks to the molds and the keel batten.

5. Check the transom to see that the centerline
on the after face of the transom aligns with the
centerline on the end-piece of the jig. If it does-
n't, check your measurements. Another check is
to draw a line perpendicular to the transom centerline and set a level to it. It should be level. The
lines you drew on the inside of the transom 7½
inches parallel to the centerline should line up
with the outside of the transom braces. If it looks
okay, drill and screw one 1½-inch drywall screw
on each side through the transom into the transom braces.

Step H: Check the rabbet and transom
bevels (Figure 30)
Now we want to make sure that the garboard
strake will fit into the rabbet along the transom,
backbone, and stem. To do this, cut a batten out
of clear pine ⅝ inch by ⅝ inch by 16 feet long. You
will need nine of these battens to line out the
planks, so you might as well make them all now.

1. If you don't have a helper, tack one end of the
batten at the top of Mold 1. Bend the batten over
the molds to the transom. Check the top part of
the transom bevel. As you finish checking that
section of the transom, move the batten down at
Mold 1. Check the bevel and correct with your
spokeshave as you go. At the same time you will
be checking the after molds. Any errors should
pop out as unfair, as the batten should flow over
the molds without revealing dips, bumps, or flat
spots. If the batten shows an unfair mold, check
the setup. If the setup looks good, recheck the
mold against the drawing.

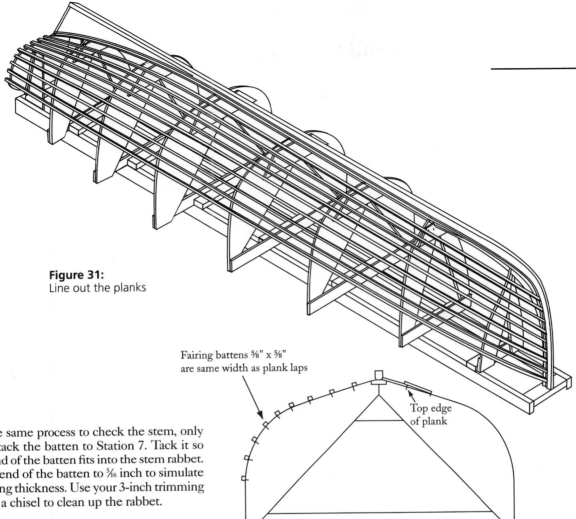

Figure 31:
Line out the planks

Fairing battens ⅝" x ⅝"
are same width as plank laps

Top edge
of plank

2. Use the same process to check the stem, only this time tack the batten to Station 7. Tack it so that the end of the batten fits into the stem rabbet. Plane the end of the batten to 5⁄16 inch to simulate the planking thickness. Use your 3-inch trimming plane and a chisel to clean up the rabbet.

3. To fair the rabbet at the keel batten and the keel, lay a straightedge along each mold and the batten. If the batten is too high, plane it off. Then lay a 6-inch-wide section of the untempered Masonite you bought for the plank template into the rabbet and tack it to the molds. Look underneath to see if it fits tightly into the rabbet and is fair. A section of planking stock should lay across the mold and keel batten, and the end should fit into the rabbet in the keel. A small rabbet plane is helpful for minor adjustments.

Step I: Line out the planks (Figure 31)
Now we will line out the planks. In this section we will determine what the plank lines will be and how the boat will look. At the same time we will determine what the plank shapes are. It is a little confusing trying to describe the planking process: As we are building the boat bottom-side up, the top of the plank on the boat is actually the bottom of the plank as we install it. When I say the top of the plank, I mean the edge of the plank that is the top edge when the boat is turned right-side up.

You will line out the plank on one side, then transfer these marks to the other side. You will need to stand off to the side and bow and stern to see the lines properly. If you are in a small space, you can move the jig around to give you the best viewing position.

1. Tack a batten through each set of the plank marks you made at the transom, Mold 4, and the stem. Your batten should be above the mark (see Figure 31). Your batten is the same width as the lap. Now eyeball your battens carefully from the top, bottom, sides, and fore-and-aft. Get down on your belly, and stand on a ladder.

Be as picky as you can. The battens should flow without noticeable twists over the molds and have even tapers. There is nothing uglier than a boat that is poorly lined out (another bummer is a boat with a lumpy or misshapen sheer). So pay particular attention to this. It is the ultimate test of a boatbuilder.

2. When you get the plank lines the way you want them on one side, mark them on the molds and transfer them to the other side.

Some people might wonder why I didn't do this step for you and line out the planks. I didn't because you need to be intimately aware what the lined-out plank should look like. As you go, you will over-plane, slightly misalign a lap, or one side will get ahead of the other. You will have to make small corrections and get back to where you belong. This is one of the key skills of a boatbuilder. If your setup is fair and the lining-out is good, you have passed the first big test.

Adjustable lap clamp

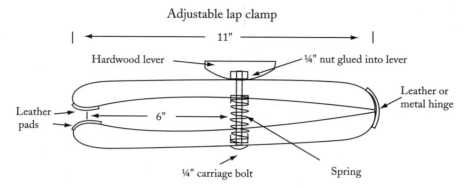

|← —————————— 11" —————————— →|

Hardwood lever ——→   ←—— ¼" nut glued into lever

Leather or metal hinge

Leather pads ——→

|← ——— 6" ——— →|

¼" carriage bolt

Spring

The clamp jaws are cut from 1½ x 1½" maple

Clothes pin clamp

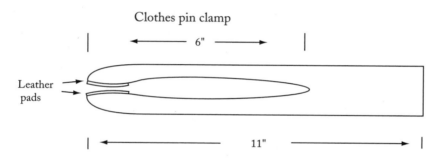

|← ——— 6" ——— →|

Leather pads ——→

|← —————————— 11" —————————— →|

Note: Can be roughly cut out of ¾" pine. Adjust clamping pressure by changing the thickness of jaws.

Modified store bought cam clamp
(6" to 8" jaw opening)

Modifications
1. Shape jaws to a slight curve and line with leather.
2. Shorten steel bar.

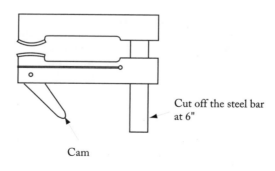

Cut off the steel bar at 6"

Cam

Figure 31A:
Homemade clamps

IV

Planking

Materials required

Planking—18 pieces white cedar flitches, Western red cedar, or Port Orford cedar, ⁵⁄₁₆ inch by 6 inches, 16 feet long (can be resawn from six pieces 8/4 by 6 inches, 16 feet long, rough).

Templates—two sheets ⅛-inch untempered Masonite or similar paneling; one sheet poster board (cardboard from art store).

Clench fastenings—⅞-inch clench nails, 3 pounds; or 1-inch copper tacks, 1½ pounds (these are approximate figures; tacks are cheaper and come more to the pound).

Bronze screws—¾-inch, 1-inch, and 1¼-inch #8, 100 of each size.

Adhesives—yellow carpenter's glue (sets up in 30 minutes); epoxy glue, 1-pint kit (for scarfing planks).

Bedding adhesive, polyurethane method—two tubes polyurethane bedding compound.

Bedding adhesive and caulking materials, traditional method—1 pint oil-based bedding compound; cotton wicking (for caulking; cotton string will work in a pinch); oil-based caulking compound.

Painting supplies—1 quart primer; 1 quart finish (interior color); one china bristle brush, 2 inches wide; 80-, 100-, and 150-grit sandpaper.

Special tools

Bucking iron—approximately 2-pound hammer head or dolly (used by auto-body repair shops).

Hammer.

Steam iron.

Hot water source—hot-water tap, stove, coffee maker.

Plastic sheeting—two sheets, each at least 2 feet by 5 feet.

Terrycloth bathroom towels or equivalent.

Assorted clamps—4-inch spring clamps, 4-inch to 6-inch C-clamps, cam clamps (see Figure 31A), 3-foot pipe clamp.

Medium-cut flat file.

The art of planking

Before you start to install planks, you have to know a few things about the bending characteristics of wood (see Figure 32). A piece of wood that is square in section will bend in two directions. As the plank gets wider, its ability to bend in both directions diminishes. Usually by the time the ratio is 2 or 3 to 1 (this will vary), the plank will only have a slight "spring" across its width. So unless the planks are very narrow, as in a strip-planked boat, or straight as in some dories and skiffs, the plank has to be cut to conform to the shape desired.

- **Materials required**
- **Special tools**
- **The art of planking**
- **Spile the garboard plank template**
- **Cut out the garboard plank**
- **Mark the gains**
- **Prepare for the next plank**
- **Plank the rest of the hull**
- **Turn over the boat**

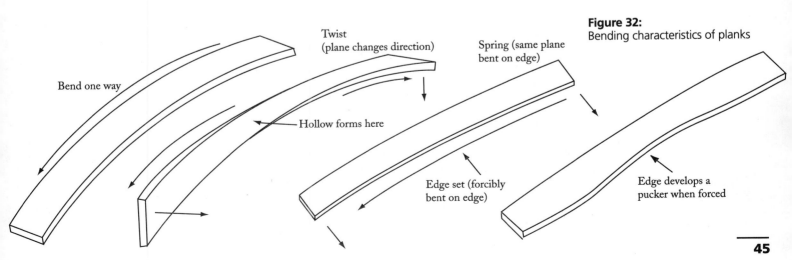

Bend one way

Twist
(plane changes direction)

Hollow forms here

Spring (same plane bent on edge)

Edge set (forcibly bent on edge)

Edge develops a pucker when forced

Figure 32:
Bending characteristics of planks

Plank Shapes (Exaggerated, not to scale)

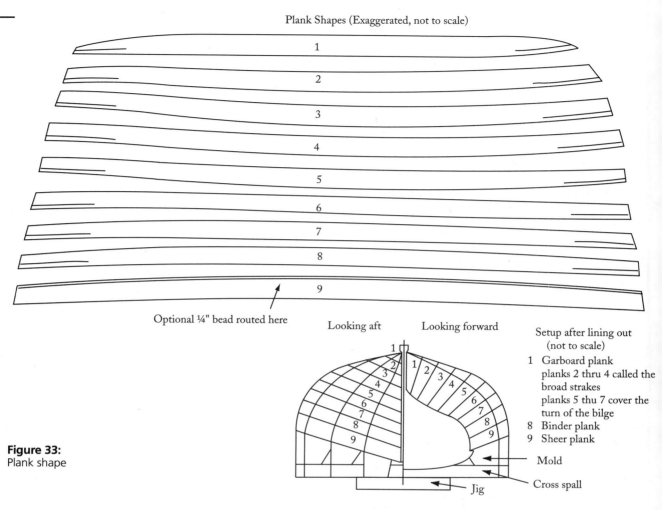

Optional ¼" bead routed here

Looking aft   Looking forward

Setup after lining out
(not to scale)

1 Garboard plank
    planks 2 thru 4 called the
    broad strakes
    planks 5 thu 7 cover the
    turn of the bilge
8 Binder plank
9 Sheer plank

Mold

Jig   Cross spall

Figure 33:
Plank shape

If you attempt to force a bend beyond the springing action, the plank will resist and pucker. Take a piece of paper and try to bend it two ways. It won't. Planking acts the same way. Forcing the plank beyond the spring is called *edge-setting* the plank. It is a good way to split planks or create ill-fitting laps. A properly planked boat has no edge-set.

Study Figure 33. When you lined out the plank, you lined it out so that the planks create fair lines along the boat. When you template those planks you will find that they are not straight at all. Most are banana-shaped and some, as they twist into the tuck of the transom, actually are S-shaped. These shapes will emerge as you template the planks.

Dry planks tend to be stiff and resist severe bending strains. In the bow and in the stern, where there is a twist, the clamping pressure required to achieve the desired shape can cause the plank to split. To avoid overly stressing the plank, wrap the end of the plank in plastic and cloth toweling and soak it with hot or boiling water, as you did with the keel batten. This will allow the plank to bend tightly into the rabbet and the tuck of the transom without splitting. Do not leave this step out. If you do, you will pay heavily!

The templates are made up out of ⅛-inch Masonite or some other thin, easily bent panel material that resists edge-setting. The templates are best made up of several smaller pieces, fastened together with butt blocks and glue (yellow carpenter's glue), and temporarily screwed and clamped until the glue sets.

It is a good idea to use the bench you made with the doors and saw horses to lay out the planks. Otherwise, you can use the floor.

If planks are damaged during the installation or fastening processes, see if you can repair the plank before you throw it away. Planks with split ends can be repaired by scarfing on new sections. For small splits around fastenings, cut open the split with a sharp knife. Cut down about ³⁄₃₂ inch and about ¹⁄₁₆ inch across. Fill with thickened epoxy.

Traditional boatbuilders did not bed the laps, and builders using that method can skip the bedding steps and go on to the next plank. Some traditionalists like to bed with oil-based bedding compound, so if you fit into that category, follow the instructions as if you were bedding with polyurethane. Be careful not to foul the caulking seams at the transom, stem, and garboard/keel seam with the oil-based compound.

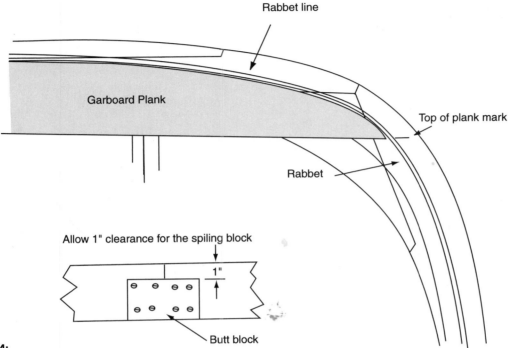

Figure 34:
The garboard template

As you add each plank, you will need to clamp them in place at the laps. As the planks are beveled, this can be tricky. In Figure 31A I show a variety of clamps that you can make to help hold the planks. The clothespin clamp is the easiest to make and use; they can be quite roughly made, as you need them. C-clamps can be used if wood pads made of scrap are placed under the jaws to protect the plank. Ingenuity is the key. Spend a little time experimenting with what you have made before you run out and spend a lot of money on clamps.

Caulking is done after the planking is completed. Run a string-sized piece of caulking material into the transom, stem, and garboard/keel seams firmly with a caulking wheel. The seam should be filled one-quarter to one-third of the depth of the seam. Be careful at the transom not to lever up the plank. With a putty knife, fill the rest of the seam with oil-based seam compound.

Those using polyurethane will not caulk and so will fill the caulking seams with polyurethane, being careful to leave a nice, even seam.

Step A: Spile the garboard plank template (Figures 33–36)

1. Study Figures 33 to 36 carefully. Thoroughly understand the process before you begin. Planking is a step-by-step process that should be followed without attempting shortcuts.

2. Cut two full-length strips (8 feet long) of your template stock, 6 inches wide. Fit one of the template pieces into the stem rabbet (Figure 34). The template should fit within ¼ inch of the rabbet in the stem and keel. Some people will eyeball the shape at the stem and trim it until it fits. I like to use poster board (cardboard) to create a pattern. I use this pattern to mark the template. It is a lot easier to fit things with a scissors and cardboard than with template material and a bandsaw.

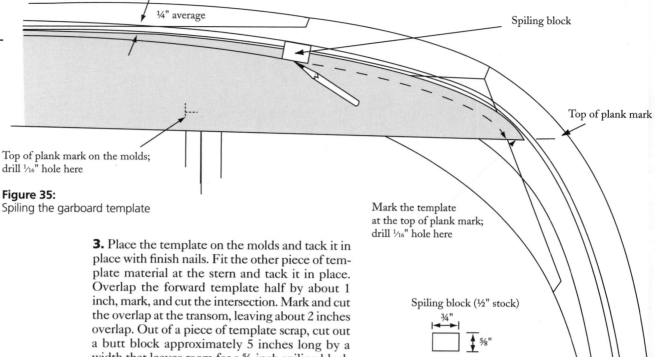

¼" average

Spiling block

Top of plank mark

Top of plank mark on the molds;
drill ¹⁄₁₆" hole here

Figure 35:
Spiling the garboard template

Mark the template
at the top of plank mark;
drill ¹⁄₁₆" hole here

Spiling block (½" stock)

¾"

⅝"

3. Place the template on the molds and tack it in place with finish nails. Fit the other piece of template material at the stern and tack it in place. Overlap the forward template half by about 1 inch, mark, and cut the intersection. Mark and cut the overlap at the transom, leaving about 2 inches overlap. Out of a piece of template scrap, cut out a butt block approximately 5 inches long by a width that leaves room for a ⅝-inch spiling block to pass at the keel. Glue the butt block over the seam in the template with yellow carpenter's glue and hold it in place with screws and clamps. The glue should set up in about 30 minutes at room temperature. The glue will not be fully cured, but it can be used if you are careful.

4. The spiling block is a small piece of wood ⅝ inch by ¾ inch by ½ inch (see Figure 35). It is used to mark a line on the template ⅝ inch parallel to the rabbet. Go ahead and mark this line on the template.

5. At the stem and transom, mark the top of plank lines on the template. At the transom, mark the template at the transom edge. On the bottom of the template, mark the plank lines from the molds.

6. Remove the template from the molds. Turn it over and drill a ¹⁄₁₆-inch hole in the top of plank line marks and the marks at stem and stern.

7. With the bandsaw, saw the line you made with the spiling block. Leave the line when you saw it out, and use your block plane to fair the template to the line.

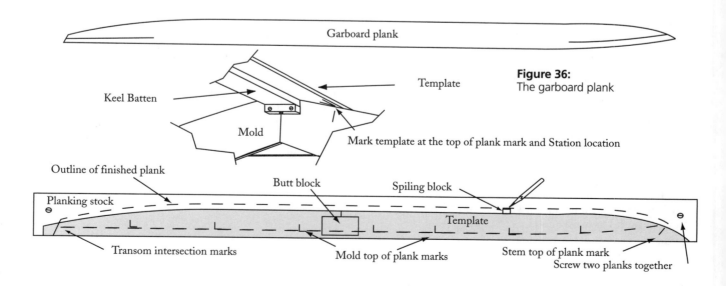

Garboard plank

Keel Batten

Mold

Template

Figure 36:
The garboard plank

Mark template at the top of plank mark and Station location

Outline of finished plank

Planking stock

Butt block

Spiling block

Template

Transom intersection marks

Mold top of plank marks

Stem top of plank mark

Screw two planks together

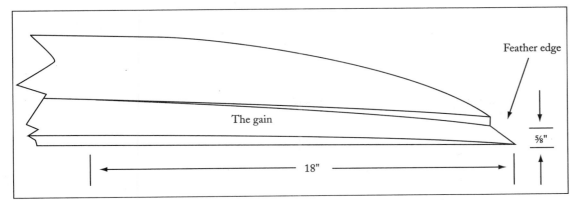

Figure 37:
The forward gains

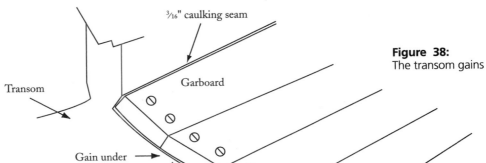

Figure 38:
The transom gains

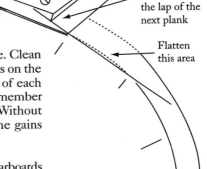

Step B: Cut out the garboard plank
(Figure 36)
The garboard is the plank or strake that is next to and fitted to the keel. In lapstrake construction, it is always the first plank to be fit. The next plank, the first broad strake, will be lapped over the garboard. Then, in sequence, each new plank will be lapped over the one that came before (see Figure 33).

1. Place the template over the planking stock. Remember to leave ⅝ inch on the keel side of the plank and about 6 inches on each end to allow for unseen splits. Clamp it to the plank. Push a pencil through the ¹⁄₁₆-inch holes at the top of plank marks. Mark the actual edge of the transom and a line 2 inches past; you will cut the 2-inch line. At the stem and keel rabbet, run the spiling block along the top of the template, marking the planking stock with a line ⅝ inch out from the template. Remove the template from the planking stock.

2. Drive nails into the pencil marks you made, marking the bottom of the plank and the plank ends at the stem and stern. Spring a fairing batten around the nails and mark the line.

3. Place the marked plank over another piece of planking stock. Put a screw at each end outside of the marked plank, securing the two planks together. You will cut out the two garboards at once. When using Eastern and Atlantic white cedar, you might have to cut out one plank and then use it as a pattern for the other. The East Coast cedars require careful navigating around sapwood, loose knots, rot, and a variety of defects. The builders that use West Coast woods on both coasts are amazed at the amount of work this can entail. On the other hand, the East Coast builders that use this stuff point to a lower board price.

4. Cut out the garboards, leaving the line. Clean up to the line with a plane. Put the planks on the molds and determine the outside faces of each plank. Mark an X on the outside face. Remember that the two planks are mirror images. Without these marks it is easy to end up with the gains (Step C) cut on the same side.

5. Mark a line on the outside face of the garboards along the stem and keel face at ³⁄₃₂ inch. Plane a bevel on this edge which goes from this line to nothing on the inside edge. This is the *expansion seam* (or the *caulking seam* if you are using the traditional method).

Step C: Mark the gains (Figures 37–38)
The *gains* are channels cut into the plank at the stem (Figure 37) and transom (Figure 38) to allow the lap of the planks to disappear at the stem and stern. You will always cut the gain at the stem on the bench, and the gain at the transom will usually be cut after the plank is fitted on the molds. The garboard is the exception to this. On the garboard both gains will be cut at the bench. The gain is 18 inches long and ⅝ inch wide.
It is best to mark the face of each pair of planks so that there will be no doubt on which side the gains will be cut. Remember, the planks are mirror images of each other. Mark the gains on both planks before you cut them. The gain is cut with a rabbet plane with an edge guide. If you don't have an edge guide, clamp a piece of wood along the gain you marked. The rabbet plane will guide on this.

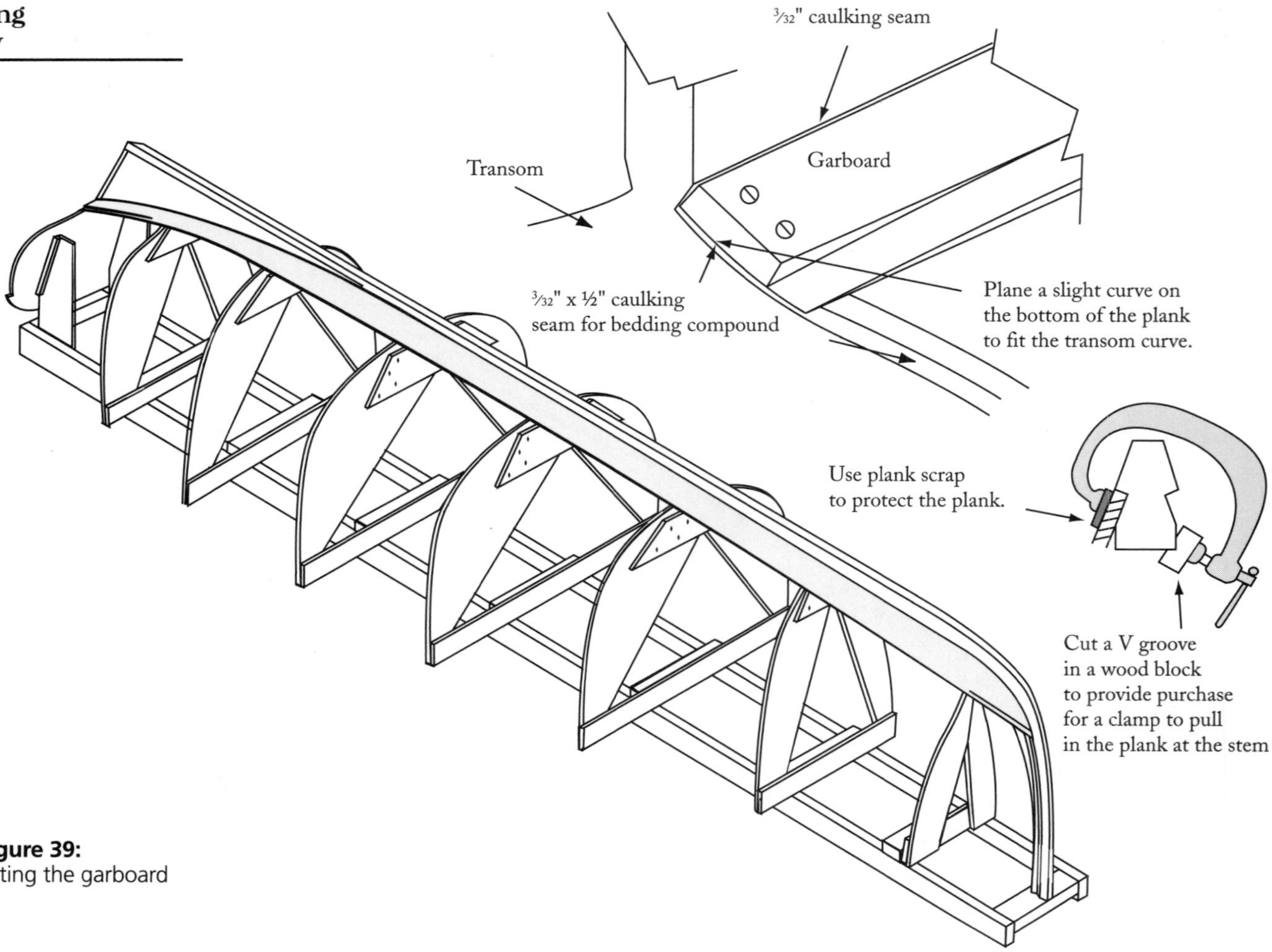

³⁄₃₂" caulking seam

Transom

Garboard

³⁄₃₂" x ½" caulking
seam for bedding compound

Plane a slight curve on
the bottom of the plank
to fit the transom curve.

Use plank scrap
to protect the plank.

Cut a V groove
in a wood block
to provide purchase
for a clamp to pull
in the plank at the stem

Figure 39:
Fitting the garboard

Step D: Fit the garboard (Figure 39)

1. Place the garboards on the molds and clamp them to the keel batten. Leave the ends free. Try to approximate the fore-and-aft placement so the planks are close to their final fitted location.

2. Apply the hot-water process to the bow and stern ends of the planks. After 10 to 15 minutes the plank should start to loosen up. Now clamp the ends in place, adding pressure as the plank starts to bend. If necessary, continue with the hot-water treatment until the plank pulls in. Let the planks set overnight.

3. Now check the fit of the plank. Touch up the fit with your block plane until the bottom edges of the planks touch the top of the plank marks on the molds and the inside edge at the keel and stem are tight, leaving a seam about ³⁄₃₂ inch at the outside edge. At the transom, round off the bottom of the plank slightly to help fit the concave shape of the transom at this point.

4. Mark and cut a ³⁄₃₂-inch expansion seam on the outer edge of the transom reaching ½ inch across the top.

5. Mark the outside edge at the transom on top of the plank. This is because the outside edge of the plank will match the angle of the transom. You will screw the transom end of the plank at an angle to keep the screws away from the edge. Using 1-inch #8 bronze screws, fasten the garboards at the stem and transom about every 1¼ inches. Allow for at least two screws in each plank at the transom. Along the keel batten, fasten every 3 inches with ¾-inch #8 screws. Do not worry if the screws break through the batten; you can file off the ends. Do not fasten in the gains! The rule is: the plank must seat firmly wood to wood before fastening. Do not pull the plank into place with screws; that will cause the plank to split. Pull it in with clamps or hand pressure before fastening. Note: If you are using the traditional method, go on to Step E. There is no bedding in the laps.

6. When everything fits, remove the screws from the forward two-thirds of the plank. Place a clamp at the point where you removed the last screw. Wedge a piece of wood under the loose end of the plank to lift it away from the rabbet. Be careful not to over-stress the plank.

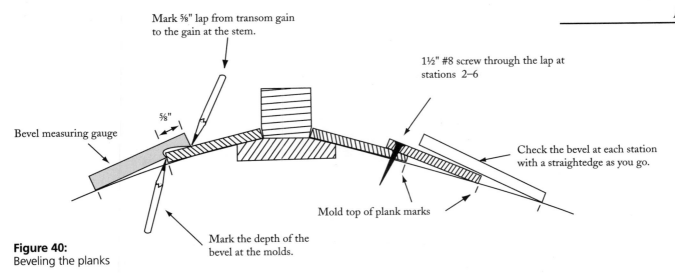

Mark ⅝" lap from transom gain to the gain at the stem.

1½" #8 screw through the lap at stations 2–6

Bevel measuring gauge

⅝"

Check the bevel at each station with a straightedge as you go.

Mold top of plank marks

Mark the depth of the bevel at the molds.

Figure 40:
Beveling the planks

7. If you are using the polyurethane method, apply a ¹⁄₁₆-inch layer of polyurethane bedding compound to the rabbet, remove the piece of wood, reclamp, and refasten. Clean up the excess polyurethane.

8. Repeat the process with the aft end of the plank. Clean up thoroughly; polyurethane bedding is practically impossible to cut out later! Use your gloves and respirator, and ventilate as much as possible. Stove alcohol or lacquer thinner will do the cleanup.

Step E: Prepare for the next plank
(Figures 40–41)

1. Cut off the plank overhang at the transom with a fine-toothed saw. Guide the saw by holding the side of the saw with your hand on the after face of the transom.

2. With the rabbet plane, make sure that the gain at the transom diminishes to a feather edge.

3. Set your combination square to ⅝ inch and draw a line along the bottom edge of the plank, marking the location of the plank lap.

4. Make a lap bevel depth gauge (see Figure 40), and mark the depth of the lap bevel at each station.

5. With your block and/or trim planes and spokeshave, carefully plane off the lap. Take long strokes, keeping an eye out for your depth marks. As you go, check the bevel at the molds with a straightedge. When you think you have it, lay a piece of template stock over several molds, clamp it, and look on the top and bottom of the lap. Make sure that it lays on the lap without gaps. Use the trim plane and spokeshave for minor corrections.

6. The lap bevel should fair nicely into the gains.

Step F: Plank the rest of the hull
(Figures 38, 41–46)
From now on you will follow the same routine.

1. At the transom, look at the shape between the plank marks. When the plank fits into a concave curve, the shape is planed on the bottom of the plank. The hot-water technique will allow for some bending across the plank, but if you try to force the plank into a concave curve, you will surely split the plank. Remember the rule that the plank must seat firmly wood-to-wood before fastening. Do not "pull in" with the screws. When the plank fits over a convex curve, you will flatten the transom between the marks. When the transom is straight under the plank, no beveling is required. Just remember to add the expansion joint bevel of ³⁄₃₂ inch by ½ inch to the transom edge.

2. Mark the ⅝-inch lap with your combination square on the last fitted plank.

3. Mark the depth of the bevel at the stations.

4. Bevel the lap, checking with a straightedge and template stock. Fair the bevel into the gains.

5. Assemble the template on the molds. It can be made of several pieces (see Figure 41). The width must allow the template to rest on the bevel and be over the plank marks on the molds. Overlap the transom 2 inches and fit into the stem rabbet within ¼ inch of the stem rabbet line. Fasten the parts together with 5-inch butt blocks held together with yellow glue and screws.

6. Use a ⅝-inch spiling block to mark the stem (see Figure 41).

7. At the transom, mark the template at the transom face and 2 inches beyond.

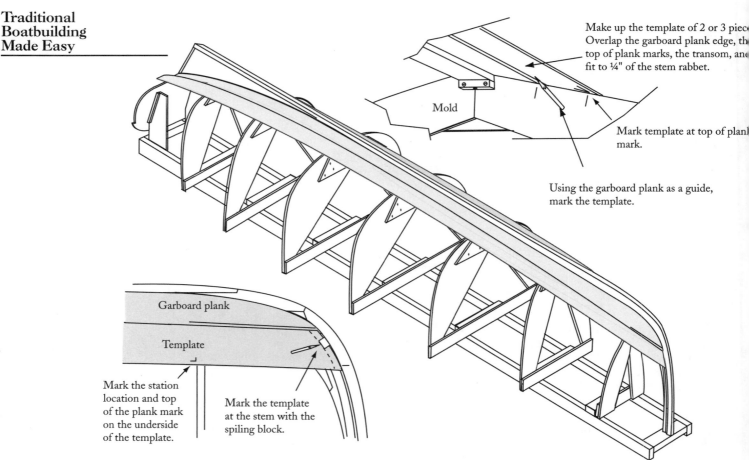

Make up the template of 2 or 3 piece Overlap the garboard plank edge, th top of plank marks, the transom, an fit to ¼" of the stem rabbet.

Mold

Mark template at top of plank mark.

Using the garboard plank as a guide, mark the template.

Garboard plank

Template

Mark the station location and top of the plank mark on the underside of the template.

Mark the template at the stem with the spiling block.

Figure 41:
Templating planks 2 through 9

8. Mark the underside of the template at the mold top of the plank marks, and make marks at stem and stern.

9. Use the last plank installed as a guide to mark the underside of the template (see Figure 41).

10. Remove the template and drill ¹⁄₁₆-inch holes at the mold top of plank marks and the marks at the stem and transom. On the bandsaw, cut on the line you made in the previous step (9).

11. Place the template over the planking stock. Leave 6 inches on each end and ⅝ inch at the top for the lap. Clamp in place.

12. If the plank is not wide enough, scarf the plank (see Figure 42):

    a. Arrange the planking stock under the template to determine the best layout of the scarf.

    b. Mark the scarf location (2½ inches long) on the template and the planking stock.

    c. Cut out the plank parts for two planks, including the 2½-inch scarf area on each plank.

    d. Stack the parts of the plank with all the scarf ends stepped 2½ inches. This will allow you to plane all the scarfs at once.

    e. Clamp the planking to a board to provide a backup to the feather edge of the scarf.

    f. Plane off the scarfs.

    g. Test the scarfed planks with the template.

    h. Block up the planking to allow clearance for clamps.

    i. Glue up the scarf and reassemble.

    j. Place plastic wrap on each side of the scarf to protect the template and blocks.

    k. Clamp the outer ends first so that the setup doesn't shift when you clamp the scarf areas.

    l. Finish clamping up.

    m. Stagger the plank scarfs on the boat so that scarfs are not near each other on succeeding planks.

13. Mark the transom end and a line 2 inches past on one piece of the planking stock (see Figure 43).

14. Mark the planking stock through the drill holes at the mold plank marks and marks at the stem and transom.

15. Moving the ⅝-inch spiling block along the stem and top edge, mark the stem and the lap side of the plank (see Figure 43).

16. Lay the marked plank over another plank and screw the two planks together at the ends outside of marked plank.

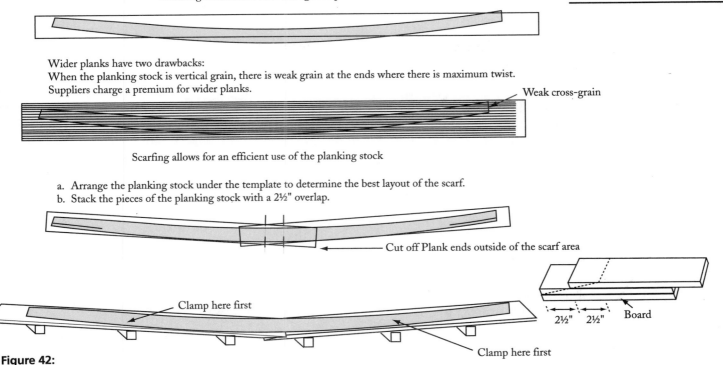

Planking stock is not wide enough for plank

Wider planks have two drawbacks:
When the planking stock is vertical grain, there is weak grain at the ends where there is maximum twist.
Suppliers charge a premium for wider planks.

Weak cross-grain

Scarfing allows for an efficient use of the planking stock

a. Arrange the planking stock under the template to determine the best layout of the scarf.
b. Stack the pieces of the planking stock with a 2½" overlap.

Cut off Plank ends outside of the scarf area

Board

2½" 2½"

Clamp here first

Clamp here first

Figure 42:
Scarfing a plank

17. Cut the planks out on the bandsaw; leave the line. Clean up to the line with your block plane.

18. Mark the gains forward and aft; they are 18 inches long and ⅝ inch wide (see Figures 37 and 38). Check the gains on the boat to ensure that they are mirror images.

19. Cut the stem gain from nothing to a feather edge. Cut a shallow (¹⁄₁₆-inch) gain at the stern. You will finish this gain on the boat after the plank is fastened.

20. Place and clamp the planks on the boat. Wrap the ends with plastic and toweling, and use the hot-water method to loosen the ends. Clamp in place overnight.

21. Fit the planks with your block plane, leaving a ³⁄₃₂-inch seam at the stem (this is beveled at the stem from nothing on the inside edge to ³⁄₃₂ inch on the outside). Be sure that the plank fits tightly into the gains. Fasten through the laps at Molds 2 through 6 with 1¼-inch #8 bronze screws (see Figure 44). Barely countersink and hand-tighten (these are temporary fastenings). There will be a frame located here. Fasten at the stem and stern with 1-inch #8 bronze screws. The stem and stern fastenings are approximately 1¼ inches apart. Do not fasten in the lower gains. On the next plank, you will put a fastening in the part of the plank that fits in the gain. Remember to account for the fore-and-aft transom bevel when installing the screws at the transom.

Figure 43:
Cutting out planks 2 to 9

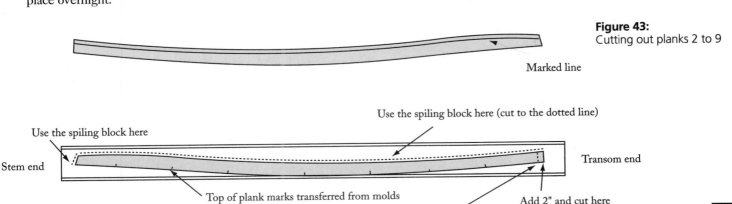

Marked line

Use the spiling block here (cut to the dotted line)

Use the spiling block here

Stem end

Transom end

Top of plank marks transferred from molds

Mark transom end

Add 2" and cut here

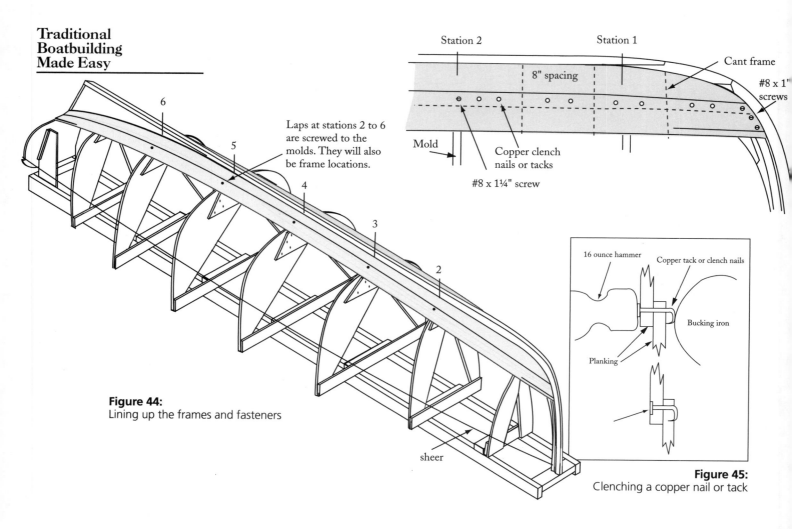

Station 2   Station 1

8" spacing

Cant frame

#8 x 1"
screws

Mold

Copper clench
nails or tacks

#8 x 1¼" screw

Laps at stations 2 to 6
are screwed to the
molds. They will also
be frame locations.

sheer

Figure 44:
Lining up the frames and fasteners

16 ounce hammer

Copper tack or clench nails

Bucking iron

Planking

Figure 45:
Clenching a copper nail or tack

22. Mark the frame locations at 8-inch centers at the keel. There are two frames between each mold at Stations 2 through 6 and one on each mold. They will spread out slightly as they reach the sheer. The three frames forward of Mold 2 and aft of Mold 7 are *canted*— that is, they splay out to avoid the appearance of bending aft. This effect is created by the greater distance around the sheer. None of these frames fall on Mold 1 or 7. As you add each plank, spring a light batten through the frame marks on the planks to ensure that they are aligned before you drill any holes.

23. Mark for the clench fastenings (⅞-inch clench nails, or 1-inch tacks). There are two in each bay between the frames and in the upper gains to within 6 inches of the ends (see Figure 44). Divide the spaces between the frames evenly; clench fastenings cannot fall at the frame locations.

24. Drill pilot holes for the clench fastenings (do a test first on scrap); they should be a hammer fit through the pilot hole.

25. Release the clamps and screws on the forward two-thirds of the plank. Clamp at the end of the loose plank. Wedge the plank lap open. Apply polyurethane bedding on the lap, 1/16 inch thick tapering to nothing at the bottom of the lap. Reclamp, refasten with screws, and clench the lap.

As you hammer each copper tack or clench nail through its pilot hole, place the bucking iron under the plank set at an angle so that the point of the fastening bends into a hook as you hammer. The tip of the hook will re-enter the plank and act as a staple (see Figure 45). After the point re-enters the plank, push the iron flat on the inside of the plank and hammer the head of the fastener until it is flush with the top of the plank. Don't worry if there are "dimples" in the wood, but don't get too carried away as you hammer. Clean up the polyurethane adhesive immediately with alcohol, lacquer thinner, or acetone, wearing your respirator and gloves.

26. Repeat the process with the stern half of the plank. Then do the other side.

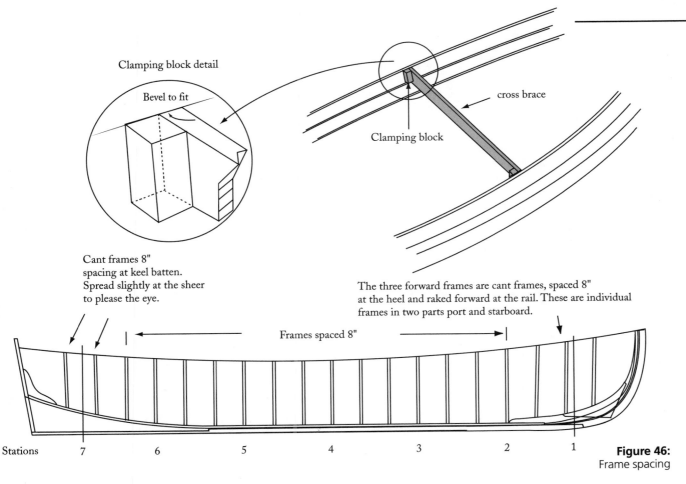

Clamping block detail

Bevel to fit

cross brace

Clamping block

Cant frames 8"
spacing at keel batten.
Spread slightly at the sheer
to please the eye.

The three forward frames are cant frames, spaced 8"
at the heel and raked forward at the rail. These are individual
frames in two parts port and starboard.

Frames spaced 8"

Stations   7   6   5   4   3   2   1

Figure 46:
Frame spacing

27. Cut off the plank flush with the transom; use a fine-toothed handsaw. Guide the cut by holding the side of the saw against the aft face of the transom as you saw.

28. To pull out the dimples, place a piece of water-soaked toweling over each clench fastening head. With a household steam iron or a soldering iron, apply heat until steam rises from the towel. Repeat until the dimple disappears.

29. Check with your finger for clench nail or tack heads that protrude above the surface. If the head protrudes too much, reset it with your hammer and bucking iron. Otherwise, use a file to grind it flush.

30. To mark the gain at the transom (Figure 38), mark the transom shape under the next plank. This shape will fair into the gain of the plank you just installed. Mark a straight line on the aft face of the transom to line out what has to be flattened, and continue this line over the end of the gain in the last plank fitted. This will give you the bevel of the gain required. With your rabbet plane, plane the gain to the required shape. Plane off the transom and add the expansion joint of ³⁄₃₂ inch by ½ inch.

31. Wrap some 100-grit sandpaper around a block of wood, and sand the plank.

32. Repeat the whole process with the next pair of planks.

33. The process is the same with the sheerstrake, except that the sheerstrake has no gains cut into it.

34. A common detail at the sheerstrake is to rout a ¼-inch bead, a half-round detail that will later be painted a contrasting color, along the bottom edge of the plank. This can be done on the bench with a router bit. You will have to increase the lap by to 1 inch to allow for the bead and the lap fastenings.

35. Pilot-drill for the frame fastenings, except for the cant frames (see Figure 46), with a drill/countersink. Countersink lightly, as the fastenings will pull in deeper in the soft cedar. The size of the drill can be determined by placing it over the screw. You should clearly see the screw threads but not the shank of the screw. Be sure to hold the drill so that it is perpendicular-to-tangent to the hull. You can make a jig to get this right by drilling a hole through a piece of ½-inch oak with a drill press and starting the drill/countersink through it.

Step G: Turn over the boat (Figure 50)

1. To prepare for turning over, unscrew Molds 1, 3, 5, and 7 from the planks, keel, and jig, and remove them. Unscrew the transom, stem, and Molds 2, 4, and 6 at the jig. These molds will remain in the boat until a cross brace is fitted.

2. Pull the boat off of the jig and place it upright on the floor. Block it off the floor until it is at a comfortable height so that you can work on the inside. You can use saw horses with short legs for this. Clamp lengths of wood to the sheer and transom to act as legs to hold the boat upright, or wedge pieces of wood (wrapped in toweling to protect the planking) between the boat and the saw horses.

3. Just aft of Mold 4, install a cross brace of 1-inch by 4-inch pine or the equivalent (see Figure 46). Screw 1½-inch by 1½-inch by 4-inch clamping blocks to the cross brace at each end and clamp it to the sheerstrake. Bevel the clamping blocks to fit. Pad the clamping block and the end of the cross brace with cloth or folded-over paper to protect the plank surfaces.

4. Unscrew and remove the remaining molds.

5. Clean up the inside. Clench any clench fastenings you couldn't reach before and sand lightly. Pull the hammer dimples by steaming as you did the outside. Sand the surface lightly.

6. Prime and paint the inside. Use a good-quality marine paint primer or the equivalent for the first coat. Thin the first primer coat the maximum allowed by the manufacturer. Then apply one coat of primer and one coat of finish laced with one-third primer (you can approximate this) and thin both coats 10 percent or until they flow without drag. Use finish paint and primer from the same manufacturer and read the label carefully. Use a good-quality 2-inch china bristle brush. If the paint supplier can tint the primer to approximate the finish color, have it done. See Chapter VIII for a further discussion of the painting process.

V

Framing

In this section you will stiffen up the boat with frames, breasthook, and quarter knees. You will learn how to steam-bend and how to fit complex parts.

Materials required

Frames—flat-grained green, clear white oak bending stock. You will need 19 frames for the boat plus extras—say, 28 frames ⅝ inch by ¾ inch, 8 feet long. You can get this out of four pieces of oak 4/4 by 7 inches. Figure on ⅞ inch (flat-grain dimension) by ¾ inch by 8 feet long (rough) for each frame.

Breasthook and quarter knees—¾-inch Honduras mahogany, white oak, fir.

Bronze wood screws—1¼-inch #8 bronze screws, 100.

Steam box (see Step C, Figure 51)

Box sides—two pieces 2-inch by 6-inch (1½ inches by 5½ inches, 8 feet long, finished) construction-grade fir, pine, or hemlock; ⅜-inch C/D exterior plywood 9 inches wide by 8 feet long.

Fastenings—¼-inch drywall screws (steel self-tapping drywall screws or the equivalent), 100.

Box interior rack—½-inch hardwood dowel, 3 feet long (to keep the frames up off the bottom of the box).

Steam source—25-cubic foot propane tank and hose; cast-iron burner, crab cooker, grass burner, camp stove, or equivalent; 5-gallon clean, empty steel fuel, solvent, or paint can, or any other steel container of a similar size with a small opening; 6-inch to 1-foot rubber hot-water (auto heater) hose to fit in the can opening.

Step A: Make and install the knees
(Figures 47–49)

Before installing the frames, you will stiffen up the boat so that you don't put any stress on the plank intersections with the stem and transom. This will be done by installing the breasthook at the stem (see Figures 47 and 48) and the quarter knees at the transom (see Figure 49). Some care should be taken in designing the shapes of these parts, as they are critical to the artistry of the boat. Along with the plank layout, shape of the sheer, transom shape, and stem profile, the shape of the quarter knees and breasthook determine the "look" of the boat. Lumpy, ugly knees are a sure sign of an amateur.

These parts are critical in the structure of the boat. They will be cut out of ¾-inch stock. Honduras mahogany is my favorite for this, with fir or some other strong softwood a good substitute. Oak is my last choice. Even small amounts of oak add dramatically to the weight of the boat, so I like to stay away from it unless absolutely necessary for structural reasons.

Use poster board to plan out the knees and the breasthook. Leave enough width at the sides to allow the inwale to fair into the knees and the breasthook. There will be a slight bevel on the inner face of the knee and the breasthook to allow the inwale to fair smoothly and for appearance.

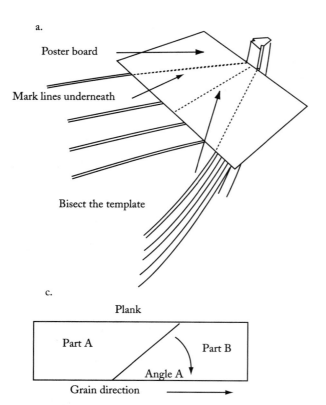

a.

Poster board

Mark lines underneath

Bisect the template

b.

5"

Angle A

Pattern

11"

End dimension 1⅜"

Splines are best
made of ¼" plywood,
but next best choice is flat grain
plank. Never use vertical
grain plank for a spline.

d.

Grain direction

Grain direction

Part A

Part B

Spline

c.

Plank

Part A

Part B

Angle A

Grain direction

Figure 47:
Making the breasthook

1. To make the breasthook (Figure 47–49), place a piece of poster board over the bow up against the stem (Figure 47a). The poster board should be long enough to cover 11 inches of the top of the planks from the stem. Mark the poster board with the outline of the inside of the plank and the aft side of the stem. Cut out this pattern.

2. Cut the pattern down the centerline (Figure 47b).

3. Cut the stock you will use (Figure 47c). Plane the cut edges smooth and fit them together. When the pieces are fit together, the grain should run parallel with the outside of the breasthook. The pattern for the breasthook should fit comfortably on this assembly.

4. Use a ¼-inch slot-cutting router or a table saw to cut the ¼-inch slots for a 1-inch-wide spline (Figure 47d). The slots will be ½ inch deep. Glue up the breasthook.

5. Mark the pattern on the breasthook stock.

6. Place a board across the top of the sheerstrakes about 5 inches aft of the stem (Figure 48e). Place your bevel gauge on the board at 90 degrees to the sheerstrake on one side. Record this bevel on a piece of scrap. Check the bevel at the other side. If it is different, record this bevel too. Then pick up the bevel at the stem the same way. Set these bevels on the bandsaw, and cut out the breasthook (Figure 48f).

7. On the pattern, lay out the inside shape of the breasthook to suit your eye. Leave about 5 inches of material from the stem and 1⅜ inches at the ends (Figure 48g). It is best not to cut this out on the bandsaw until framing is complete and you are fitting the inwale.

8. Fit and fasten the breasthook in place with 1-inch #8 screws. Do not bed this, as it is easier to remove the breasthook and finish it on the bandsaw after framing.

e.

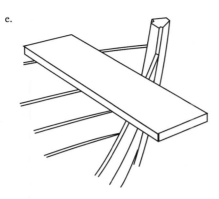

f.

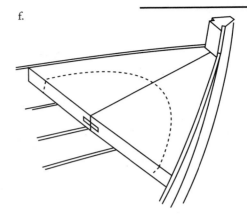

g.

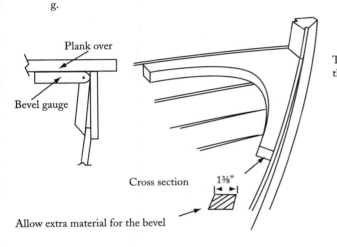

Plank over

Bevel gauge

Cross section   1⅜"

Allow extra material for the bevel

h.

The inwale will fair into
the breasthook like this

Figure 48:
Making the breasthook
(continued)

9. To make the quarter knees, take a piece of poster board approximately 7 inches by 11 inches and place it over the sheerstrake and against the transom. The poster board should angle up away from the sheerstrake slightly (Figure 49).

10. Mark the underside of the pattern at the sheerstrake. The straight edge at the transom will be the aft line of the quarter knee. With your scissors, cut the line.

11. Place the pattern on the boat, and take off the bevels at the transom and the plank. Mark the shape of the curved inside of the knee on the pattern with a 1-inch radius at the transom and leaving 1¼ inches at the plank end.

12. Mark the quarter knee on the stock as shown in Figure 49. Cut the sides on the bandsaw, and fit. Cut the inner line after you fit the inwale. Go ahead and fasten the quarter knee with 1-inch #8 screws. Do not bed.

13. Repeat this process to make the quarter knee on the other side. You can use the same pattern. Be sure that the shape and angle at the transom of the finished quarter knees are the same.

Step B: Mark the frame locations
(Figures 46, 50)

1. Mark the frame centers at 8-inch intervals along the keelson (see Figures 46 and 50).

2. At the sheer, divide the space between Stations 2-6 into three even spaces. Mark the frame centers.

3. At the turn of the bilge, divide the space again and mark the frame centers on the laps.

4. Spring a thin batten through the center points at each center mark to locate the remaining centers for each frame.

5. At each lap, place a mark ⅜ inch on each side of the center marks.

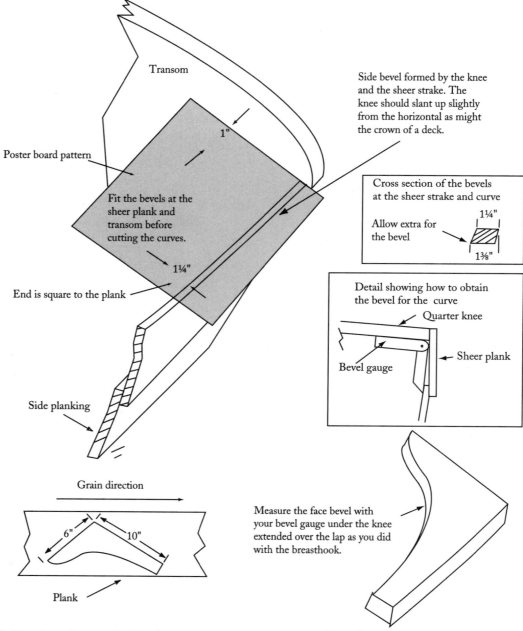

Transom

Poster board pattern

Side bevel formed by the knee
and the sheer strake. The
knee should slant up slightly
from the horizontal as might
the crown of a deck.

Fit the bevels at the
sheer plank and
transom before
cutting the curves.

1"

1¼"

End is square to the plank

Side planking

Cross section of the bevels
at the sheer strake and curve

Allow extra for
the bevel

1¼"

1⅜"

Detail showing how to obtain
the bevel for the curve

Quarter knee

Bevel gauge

Sheer plank

Grain direction

6"

10"

Plank

Measure the face bevel with
your bevel gauge under the knee
extended over the lap as you did
with the breasthook.

Figure 49:
Make and install the quarter knee

6. The three frames aft of Station 6 and three for-ward of Station 2, the cant frames, lean slightly forward. If the frames were installed parallel in these areas, the flare of the sides would make the frames appear to be bending back. To accommo-date this, the cant frames are angled forward. At the keel and stem knee, mark the frame centers at 8 inches. At the sheer the distance is greater than 8 inches; try about 9-inch spacing here. Clamp battens at these points and eyeball to check how it looks. Then mark the centerlines and the plank widths at the lap.

7. From the inside, using a ¹³⁄₃₂-inch drill, drill a hole at the centerline for each frame, centered on the lap.

8. Cut a shallow countersink. The screw will sink into the softwood, so this needs to be just a start.

9. Start 1¼-inch #8 bronze screws from the out-side until they poke through the lap.

Step C: Bending-in the frames
(Figures 51–53)

Steam-bending is one of the most feared processes. There is something mysterious about bending a stiff piece of wood as if it were a rub-ber band. After the first boat, your attitude will change. It is actually one of the simplest steps, and most find it fun. Steam-bending requires teamwork. You will need at least two people; three is better, and you can use four.

First you'll need to prepare your frame stock: Plane the plain-sawn 4/4 bending stock to ⅝ inch. Rip the bending stock on your table saw into rough-cut pieces ⅞ inch wide. Rip out extras. Depending on how much stock you bought, you should have at least 25 frames to allow for break-age. Plane this dimension to ¾ inch. This should give you frame stock ⅝ inch by ¾ inch, 8 feet long. With your block plane, round off the corners ¹⁄₁₆ inch. Keep your bending stock wet. Wrap it in plastic or soak it until you are ready to bend.

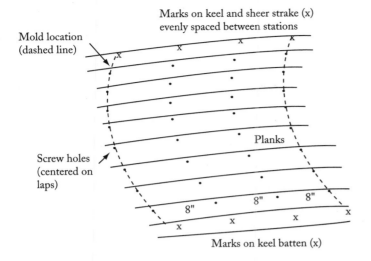

Mold location
(dashed line)

Marks on keel and sheer strake (x)
evenly spaced between stations

Screw holes
(centered on
laps)

Planks

8"   8"   8"

Marks on keel batten (x)

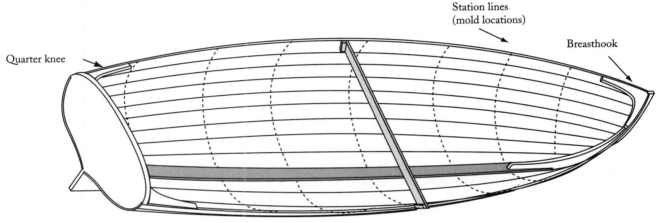

Quarter knee

Station lines
(mold locations)

Breasthook

Figure 50:
Mark frame locations

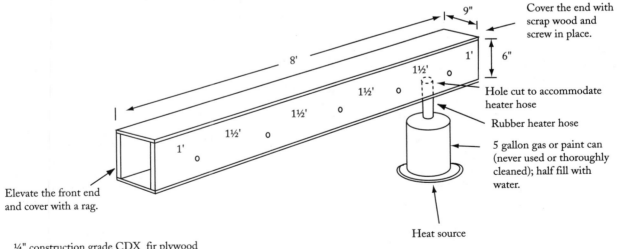

9"

Cover the end with
scrap wood and
screw in place.

8'   1'

6"

1½'

1½'   o

Hole cut to accommodate
heater hose

1½'   o

Rubber heater hose

1½'   o

5 gallon gas or paint can
(never used or thoroughly
cleaned); half fill with
water.

1'
o

Elevate the front end
and cover with a rag.

Heat source

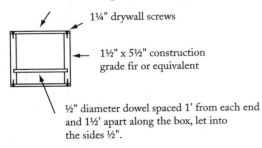

¼" construction grade CDX fir plywood

1¼" drywall screws

1½" x 5½" construction
grade fir or equivalent

Caution!

There is always the possibility of fire so
keep your heat source outside and carry
the frames inside. The frames will be hot, so wear
rubberized, heat-resistant gloves.

½" diameter dowel spaced 1' from each end
and 1½' apart along the box, let into
the sides ½".

Figure 51:
The steam box

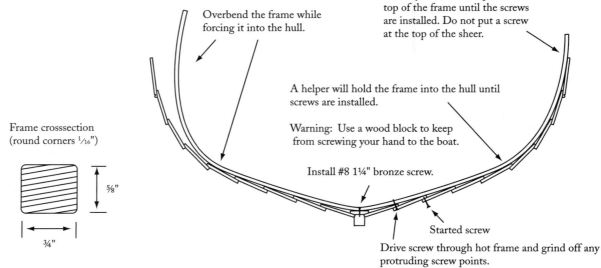

Overbend the frame while
forcing it into the hull.

Hold by hand or clamp the
top of the frame until the screws
are installed. Do not put a screw
at the top of the sheer.

A helper will hold the frame into the hull until
screws are installed.

Warning: Use a wood block to keep
from screwing your hand to the boat.

Frame crosssection
(round corners ¹⁄₁₆")

⅝"

¾"

Install #8 1¼" bronze screw.

Started screw

Drive screw through hot frame and grind off any
protruding screw points.

Figure 52:
Install the frames

The steam box is simple (see Figure 51). The frames are 8 feet long, so the box doesn't need more than this. I made my box out of wood I found around my house—two 2-inch by 6-inch fir boards (1½ inches by 5½ inches, finished) 8 feet long, and some construction-grade plywood, both left over from a construction project. This is a rough-built thing, so scrounge wherever you can. A hole is drilled at the bottom of the box about 6 inches from the end to accommodate the hot-water hose from the steam generator. The back end is plugged with a plywood cover. The other end is plugged with a rag. The pieces of ½-inch hardwood dowel, cut to fit across the box, are set ½ inch into the sides at about 1½-foot intervals about 2 inches from the bottom to keep the steam circulating around the frames.

My steam generator is a clean 5-gallon can that once held paint thinner. A new metal gas can will work, too. Fill it up about halfway. A piece of rubber radiator hose leads from the can to the box. Heat can be supplied by many sources. I have a 22-pound propane bottle attached to a burner used for a crab cooker. Inexpensive cast-iron stove elements made for propane can be found. In a pinch, a camp stove might work.

Get insulated rubber gloves to protect your hands from the hot frames. Before you begin steaming the actual frames, you need to rehearse. Use a springy oak batten ½ inch by ⅛ inch, 8 feet long, to simulate a hot frame. Here is the basic drill, with a crew of two (see Figure 52):

1. The two people stand on either side of the boat.

2. One person brings the frame to the boat and extends the frame over the boat to the second person.

3. Each person, at the same time, works his or her end of the frame into the boat, pushing the frame onto the frame location marks. Over-bend as you work the frame into the curve of the boat.

4. One person clamps their frame to the sheer to hold it and then drives a screw at the center of the keelson. This holds the middle of the frame in place.

5. This person then runs to the other side of the boat and, while the second person holds the frame in the boat, drives the screws into the hot frames; the second person uses a piece of wood to hold down the frame so he/she doesn't get screwed into the boat. No pilot hole is necessary. The screws will protrude through the frame; you will file them off after the frames are in.

6. Then the crew runs over to the other side and repeats the process. You need to be done within one minute; 30 seconds is best.

With three people, there is no need to clamp the frame. Two people hold the frame while one person installs screws. This is an improvement. With four people there is no need to switch sides. Practice your moves until you get it down cold. You will need a half hour to one hour to create steam. Have a damp terrycloth rag over the open end. Don't put more than three frames in at a time. I recommend just two; that way if you have a problem, you can't end up with overcooked frames.

When you think you are ready, put two frames in the box. They will be ready to go in about 25 minutes. Do two or three frames amidships first. Then go to the hairpins. The last two at the stern can be put in two pieces (see Figure 53). A floor can be bent in later to back this area up.

Frames at ends that are bent in one piece have a tight hairpin bend that can cause the frame to break.

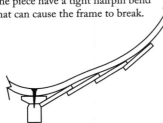

Split frames can be used if frames break at the stern. Use bent sister floors to strengthen this area. Round off the ends.

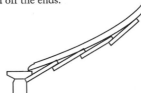

There is one split frame at the daggerboard case. Install a sister floor at the forward end of the case. Leave the ends square.

Forward of station 2 the three cant frames are split. No sister floors are required here. Note that the end is left square to prevent water and debris from collecting.

Sister floors are partial frames bent in over the keelson and two laps on each side used to add structure at split frames and near frames that have cracks at the keel batten. Place the floor about 2 inches away from the nearest frame to allow for proper ventilation and to prevent dirt from accumulating. Round off the ends.

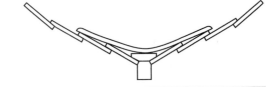

Figure 53:
Installing split frames

Sister floors (see Figures 53 and 60) are short frames crossing the keelson and two laps on each side. Install floors on each end of the daggerboard box, near frames cracked at the keelson, and at the stern if you split these frames. Mark the floor centers and widths on the laps and keelson the same way you did for the frames.

Before you actually steam, you need to rehearse. Remember that in the ends, three is a twist to the frame as well as a difficult shape near the transom, so don't skip this step. Use a springy oak batten ½ inch by ⅛ inch by 8 feet long to simulate a hot frame.

A variety of defects (see Figure 54) can pop up while steaming. Think of repairing what you can. If the defects are minor, wait until you have installed all the frames before you try to replace them, as you might run out of material.

Broken frames can be used as split frames, so leave the split frames at the ends of the boat until you have finished bending in the through frames.

After the frames are installed, cut them off, leaving 2 inches above the sheerstrake. The frames will shrink as they dry out. In some cases a frame might even pull away from the plank. If it does, you can try to reset it by removing the screws to the sheer and pulling the frame in one screw at a time. The danger with this is that you will over-stress the plank, so leave it alone if there seems to be too much pressure on the plank. Another technique is to remove the screw at the frame and put a wedge in the gap, pilot-drill through the wedge, and reinstall the screw. The last option is to leave it alone.

Now you can file off the screws penetrating the frames.

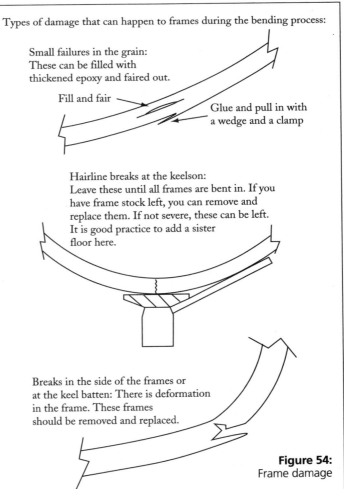

Types of damage that can happen to frames during the bending process:

Small failures in the grain: These can be filled with thickened epoxy and faired out.

Fill and fair

Glue and pull in with a wedge and a clamp

Hairline breaks at the keelson: Leave these until all frames are bent in. If you have frame stock left, you can remove and replace them. If not severe, these can be left. It is good practice to add a sister floor here.

Breaks in the side of the frames or at the keel batten: There is deformation in the frame. These frames should be removed and replaced.

Figure 54:
Frame damage

VI

Finishing Out

By now you should be an accomplished woodworker. You will learn new skills in this chapter as your boat takes its final appearance. You will take off bevels, make templates, use your handsaw to cut compound bevels, and fit compound curves. A special treat is the backrest with its carved letters and details.

Materials required

Inwales and guardrails—Honduras mahogany or white oak, ⅝ inch by 1 inch, 15 feet long.

Seat risers—Honduras mahogany, two pieces ⅝ inch by 2¼ inches, 13 feet long.

Floorboards—cedar, one piece ⅝ inch by 2½ inches, 10 feet long; four pieces ⁵⁄₁₆ inch by 5½ inches, 10 feet long.

Drain plug—one, plastic (available at any marine chandlery).

Thwarts, horseshoe seat—white cedar, Western red cedar, or Port Orford cedar, ¾ inch by 9 inches (8 and 7 inches, finished), two pieces 14 and 12 feet long.

Turned posts—two, made of 1½-inch by 1½-inch by 9-inch stock. Can be bought at a home-improvement store, or you can turn them yourself on a lathe (or hand-shape them with a rasp and chisel).

Thwart knees—Honduras mahogany, ¾ inch by 6 inches, 4 feet long.

Backrest (optional)—Honduras mahogany, ¾ inch by 9½ inches, 34 inches long.

Oarlock pads—scrap pieces of Honduras mahogany or oak.

Step A: Fit the inwales
(Figures 55 and 57)

1. On the frames that begin 2 feet from the transom to 2 feet from the stem, mark a level line at the sheer. Use a straightedge laid across the boat. Then, on each frame mark a beveled line. From the sheer to the inside of the frame, the rise of the line is ¹⁄₁₆ inch (see Figure 55a).

2. Cut the inwales out of ⅝-inch by ⅞-inch stock. Fitting one inwale at a time, clamp each inwale on the inside of the frames on top of the marks and on top of the quarter knee and the breasthook. Put enough clamps on the inwale to prevent gaps between the inwale and the frames. Overlap the knee and breasthook by at least ⅞ inch.

3. Mark the overlap on the inwale and mark the bevel on the end. The bevel goes from a ⅞-inch overlap on the inside to a ¾-inch overlap at the outside (see Figure 55). Draw a line on the inside face of the inwale that is square to the top. Using a dovetail saw, cut the ends, leaving the inwale clamped in place. Start your saw cut at the top inside corner, tracking down the face and the top lines at the same time. Make sure that the end is square to the top. If it isn't, loosen the clamps and use your block plane to square it up.

4. Using a sharp pencil, trace around the forward end of the inwale onto the breasthook and draw a line down the face of the breasthook square to the top. Use the inwale as a guide to cut this line, again using the dovetail saw.

5. Loosen the forward clamps and push the inwale into the notch you just cut. Tap with a hammer at the aft end of the inwale until the forward end fits tightly. If there are slight gaps, run your saw through the joint and lightly hammer the end. Repeat this until the joint is tight.

- **Materials required**
- **Fit the inwales**
- **Shape and fit the guardrails**
- **Install the seat risers**
- **Install the horseshoe seat brace**
- **Fit the keelson and floorboards**
- **Install the drain plug**
- **Fit the horseshoe seat**
- **Fit the forward center thwart and daggerboard case**
- **Fit the forward thwart, mast partners, and maststep**
- **Fit the thwart knees**
- **Fit the oarlock pads**
- **Fit the backrest**
- **Carve the boat name and decorative details**

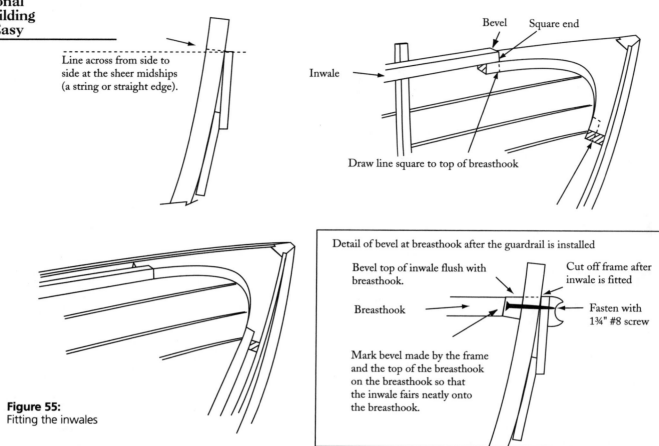

Line across from side to
side at the sheer midships
(a string or straight edge).

Bevel   Square end

Inwale

Draw line square to top of breasthook

Detail of bevel at breasthook after the guardrail is installed

Bevel top of inwale flush with
breasthook.

Cut off frame after
inwale is fitted

Breasthook

Fasten with
1¾" #8 screw

Mark bevel made by the frame
and the top of the breasthook
on the breasthook so that
the inwale fairs neatly onto
the breasthook.

Figure 55:
Fitting the inwales

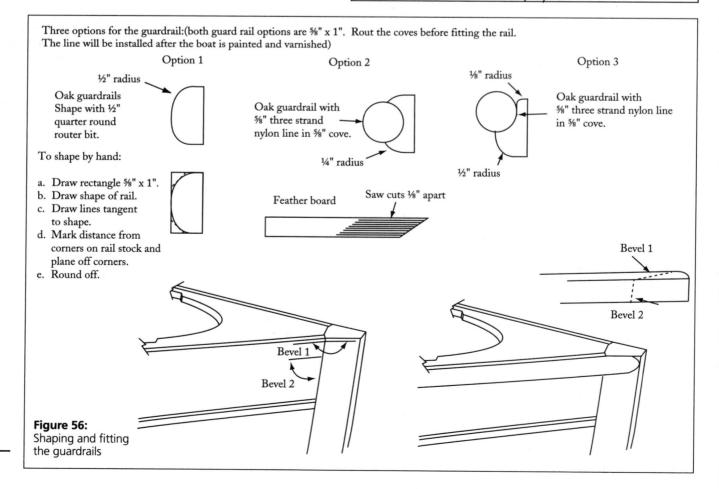

Three options for the guardrail:(both guard rail options are ⅝" x 1". Rout the coves before fitting the rail.
The line will be installed after the boat is painted and varnished)

Option 1

½" radius

Oak guardrails
Shape with ½"
quarter round
router bit.

To shape by hand:

a. Draw rectangle ⅝" x 1".
b. Draw shape of rail.
c. Draw lines tangent
   to shape.
d. Mark distance from
   corners on rail stock and
   plane off corners.
e. Round off.

Option 2

Oak guardrail with
⅝" three strand
nylon line in ⅝" cove.

¼" radius

Option 3

⅛" radius

Oak guardrail with
⅝" three strand nylon line
in ⅝" cove.

½" radius

Feather board

Saw cuts ⅛" apart

Bevel 1

Bevel 2

Bevel 1

Bevel 2

Figure 56:
Shaping and fitting
the guardrails

6. At the aft end, use a pencil to mark the outline of the inwale overlap on each quarter knee and draw a line on the face square to the top. You will leave the pencil lines when you cut the top line. You can use the inwale to guide the line at the back of the inwale, but you will have to lift the inwale end to cut the top line. Leave the clamps at the forward end and remove the clamps at the aft end. Cut the top line carefully. It will fit best if you cut it right the first time.

7. Lower the inwale into the notch. If necessary, improve the fit with the dovetail saw as you did with the forward end. A slight gap (1/16 inch) is all right, as you need room for expansion. Make sure that the inwale fairs nicely into the curve of the breasthook and the quarter knees.

8. After everything fits, remove the inwales and set them aside.

Step B: Shape and fit the guardrails
(Figures 55–57)

There are three options for the guardrail, as shown in Figure 56. The first is a solid white oak rail, 5/8 inch by 1 inch, rounded off with a plane or a 1/2-inch corner-round router bit. The second and third options include a 5/8-inch three-strand nylon rope fender (installed after the boat is varnished or painted; see Chapter VIII, Figure 83). To cut a groove for the rope, you need to rout a 5/8-inch cove into the guardrail. If you have a router table, routing the cove in the center of the rail (option two) is possible. Otherwise (option three), you can rout a corner off the guard stock with a 5/8-inch router bit, holding the router by hand. This does not hold the rope as firmly as second option, but it will work.

To cut the center cove for option two, you need to hold the stock into the router bit snugly; otherwise, it will jump around, ruining the cut. You can either buy or make a router table. If you have a particle-board extension table on your table saw, as I do, you can transform it into a router table by installing a plastic router-table insert (see Figure 56A). The insert can either be bought from a tool supplier, or made out of a 9-by-12-inch piece of 1/4-inch polycarbonate (Lexan is one trademark). Cut a hole in the extension table 1/2 inch smaller than the outside shape of the insert, and use a 1/2-inch rabbet router bit to cut a shelf that your insert sets on. For the 5/8-inch cove bit, cut a 1-inch hole in the center of the insert (larger if you use larger-radius bits), replace the plastic base on your router with the table insert, install the router bit, and you are all set. You can make a fence by clamping a piece of wood 1 1/2 inches by 2 1/2 inches by the width of your table. As for the router itself, it need not be that expensive. I have a 1 3/4-horsepower router made by the Skill company that I regularly see on sale for less than $75. There may be an advantage to spending a little more for a router

that will hold a 1/2-inch shank, as this will give you the capability to use heavy-duty router bits.

You'll also need some feather boards to hold the stock down (see Figure 56A). Feather boards can be bought at the same place you bought the router base, but they are easy to make yourself. Starting with pieces of stock 3/4 inch by 2 inches, 1 foot long, saw (on the bandsaw) a series of parallel cuts 1/8 inch apart and about 6 inches deep. Then cut a bevel on the cut end. When you clamp the uncut end to the fence, forcing the cut end onto the stock you are routing, the feather board will act like a spring, holding the stock down while allowing it to move freely.

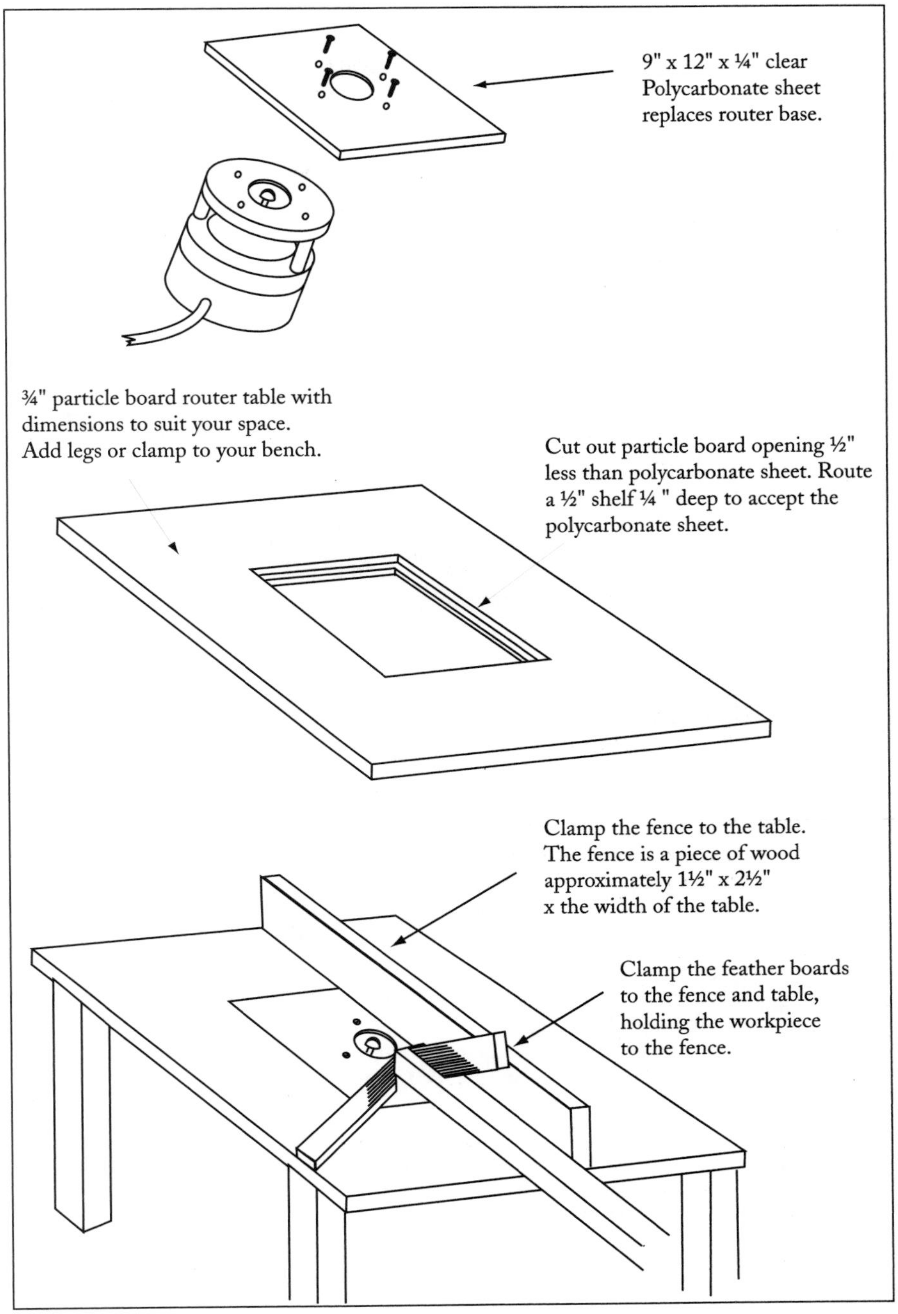

9" x 12" x 1/4" clear Polycarbonate sheet replaces router base.

3/4" particle board router table with dimensions to suit your space. Add legs or clamp to your bench.

Cut out particle board opening 1/2" less than polycarbonate sheet. Route a 1/2" shelf 1/4" deep to accept the polycarbonate sheet.

Clamp the fence to the table. The fence is a piece of wood approximately 1 1/2" x 2 1/2" x the width of the table.

Clamp the feather boards to the fence and table, holding the workpiece to the fence.

Figure 56A:
Router table

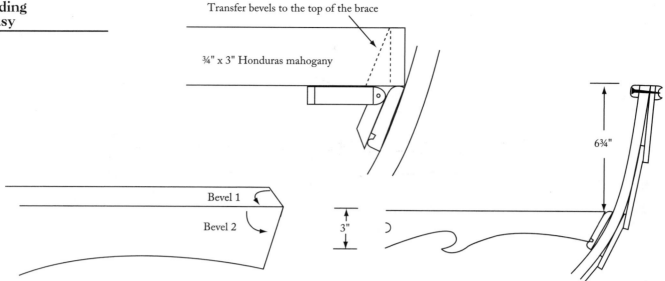

Transfer bevels to the top of the brace

¾" x 3" Honduras mahogany

Bevel 1

Bevel 2

3"

6¾"

Figure 57:
Install riser and
horseshoe seat brace

1. From your 4/4 white oak stock, cut out and finish two guardrails ⅝-inch by 1-inch, 15 feet long (see Figure 56). Shape the guardrails to one of the options that I have suggested.

2. The guardrail needs a compound cut at the stem to fit into the bevel made by the intersection of the sheerstrake and the stem. Take the first bevel at the top of the sheerstrake and the stem (see Figure 56). The second bevel is the line at the top of the top of the sheer and the line made by the intersection of the forward end of the sheerstrake and the stem. Mark these bevels on the stock, and cut with your fine-toothed saw. Fit with your block plane if you have to. You probably have figured out by now that the best solution to the problem is to accurately measure the bevels and cut them right on. A little practice cutting lines on spare stock will pay off handsomely in the speed of fitting these joints.

3. The rails are fastened from the inside through the inwale, frame, and sheerstrake into the guardrail with 1¾-inch #8 screws, as shown in Figures 55 (inset) and 57. If you are rounding-over the edges (option one) and planning to varnish the rail, 1½-inch screws will do. Use a countersink that pre-drills a hole for a ⅜-inch plug (bung). At the same time that you buy this countersink, buy a matching plug cutter. After the rails are installed, you'll bed the end of each plug with glue and tap it into the hole with the grain running in the same direction of the grain in the rails.

If you plan to paint the rails, you need only countersink enough to putty the hole with some sort of exterior wood filler. Pilot-drill and install one screw at the stem and two through the breasthook. Remove the screws and the guardrail. Dry-fit the rails and pilot-drill for and install all screws. When everything fits well, cut off the aft ends of the guardrails flush with the transom, with a slight bevel angling forward. Remove the rails and sand with 100-grit sandpaper.

4. Bed with an acrylic latex bedding compound the full length of the guardrail and the ends of the inwale where they fit into the knees and breasthook, and refasten. Clean up thoroughly, right away.

5. Cut off the frame ends with your handsaw, using the rails as a guide. With a block plane and a sander, fair the top of this assembly. A belt sander with a 100-grit belt, if carefully used, works well here. Remember that you can do a lot of damage with this tool, so proceed carefully. A more conservative approach would be to make a flexible sanding board about 2 feet long out of ¼-inch plywood. Cut and attach a 100-grit sanding belt with contact cement. This is an excellent fairing tool.

Step C: Install the seat risers
(Figures 57, 58, and 60)
The seat risers are made from ⅝-inch by 2¼-inch stock. Round over the top by hand or with a ½-inch quarter-round router bit. The bottom can be rounded or beaded. Beading is a traditional touch. The old-timers had hand planes for this job, but you can buy a router bit from some of the mail-order tool companies.

The riser overlaps the second frame from each end by 2 inches. The top of the riser is 6¾ inches below the sheer at the stern and amidships and 7½ inches at the forward end. Install a 1¼-inch #8 screw at each frame. You don't have to bed the riser.

Locate the thwart locations on the tops of the risers (see Figure 60): The two center thwarts are finished 8 inches wide, and the forward thwart is 9½ inches wide. The after edge of the forward center thwart is 34 inches forward of the daggerboard case. The aft edge of the forward thwart butts against the forward end of the centerboard case. The after edge of the aft center thwart is 38 inches from the after edge of the forward center thwart.

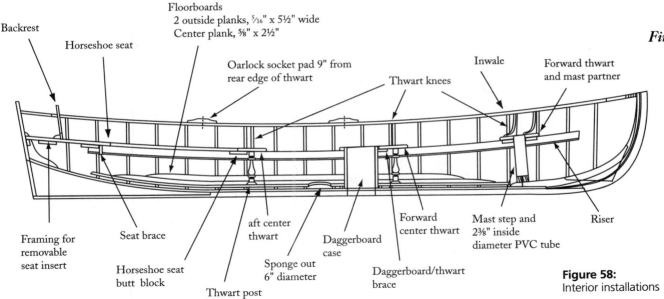

Backrest

Horseshoe seat

Floorboards
2 outside planks, 5/16" x 5½" wide
Center plank, 5/8" x 2½"

Oarlock socket pad 9" from
rear edge of thwart

Thwart knees

Inwale

Forward thwart
and mast partner

Framing for
removable
seat insert

Seat brace

Horseshoe seat
butt block

Thwart post

aft center
thwart

Sponge out
6" diameter

Daggerboard
case

Daggerboard/thwart
brace

Forward
center thwart

Mast step and
2⅜" inside
diameter PVC tube

Riser

Figure 58:
Interior installations

Step D: Install the horseshoe seat brace (Figure 57)

You are by now a pro at cutting a compound bevel, so here's a test: Take a piece of Honduras mahogany ¾ inch by 3 inches with enough length to reach across the risers and place it ¾ inch forward of the second-to-last frame at the stern on top of the riser. With your combination square set at 3 inches, measure square from the top of the seat brace to the top inside edge of the riser. Mark the top of the stock at this point. With your bevel gauge, measure the bevel formed by the intersection of the face of the brace and the riser, and a second bevel at the intersection of the brace and the riser at the top (see Figure 57). Mark these bevels on the brace stock at the point you located, and repeat the process on the other side of the brace. Cut the lines with your handsaw, and fit the brace with your block plane.

Remove the brace, and shape the bottom edge. Design your own shape for the bottom of the brace; we are looking for a design that is reminiscent of Victorian times. Sand and bed with acrylic latex compound, and fasten the brace to the riser.

Step E: Fit the keelson and floorboards (Figure 59)

1. The keelson, or center "floorboard," is ⅝ inch by 2½ inches. The forward section starts at the stem knee and butts at the daggerboard case on a floor timber. The aft section is butted against the after end of the daggerboard case and extends to 2 inches beyond the second-to-last frame. The ends are squared. At the stern there is a bend over the deadwood. Pre-bend this area with hot water: Using the jig you made for the keel batten, wrap the after end of the floorboard in plastic and toweling, soak with boiling water, bend it over this jig, and let it set.

2. The next boards (5½ inches by 5/16 inch) are fitted tightly to the keelson. They extend 4 inches beyond the next frames in from the stem and stern. There is a rounded taper at each end, starting from a 2½-inch radius, for 12 inches fore-and-aft. The outer set of floorboards extend 4 inches beyond the next frames in, and have the same taper at the ends, beginning just aft of the taper of the first set. Use your own judgment, based on how things look, and feel free to make adjustments. Before you fit the floorboards, mark on the riser the locations of the 'thwartship seats (see Figures 58, 60, 61, and 62). You want to be sure that you don't put screws through the floorboards under the seats; this would complicate removal of the floorboards for refinishing.

To fit the floorboards tight, push the next board up against the installed board and set a pencil compass to the largest gap and move it along the board, marking a line. Plane to this line and fit again. When it fits, round the edge 1/16 inch with sandpaper. There is no bedding in this installation. Install the floorboards with ¾-inch #8 screws. Between the first frame aft of the daggerboard case and the next, draw a 6-inch-diameter circle for the sponge-out hole. Remove the floorboards and cut the circle. Sand the edges and reinstall.

Drain plug detail

Eliptically shaped block

Profile view

Bottom view

Drain plug

Garboard plank

Eliptically shaped block

SEE ADENDUM.

Drain plug

3' 1"

2' 4½"

2' 10"

Taper from 2½" radius for 12"

Keelson

Floorboards

6" sponge out

Daggerboard case

Mast tube

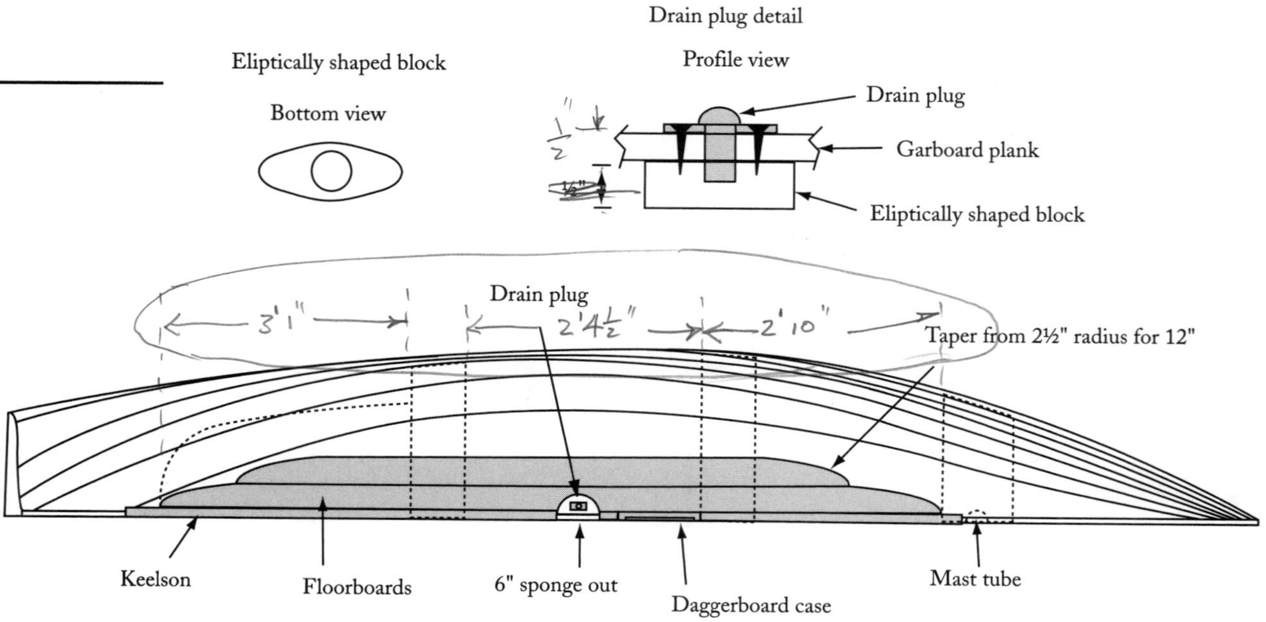

Figure 59:
Floorboards, keelson,
and drain plug

Step F: Install the drain plug
(Figure 59)

A drain plug is installed in such a way that it can be opened from within the sponge-out hole. A ½-inch-thick elliptically shaped block of Honduras mahogany is installed on the outside of the boat to receive the ends of the ¾-inch screws holding the drain plug (see Figure 59). This exact shape of the block depends on the drain plug. Be sure and shape the block so that it minimizes water resistance.

Step G: Fit the horseshoe seat
(Figures 58, 60, 61)

Before you begin to build the horseshoe seat, study the drawings so that you thoroughly understand what you are going to do.

1. To locate the horseshoe seat cleat at the transom, place a straightedge on top of the riser and extend it until it touches the transom, about 1 inch from the side. Record the bevel made by the straightedge and the transom. Mark this point on both sides; you will draw a line between the two marks. Since the transom knee is in the way, you can make a measuring tool with a straight piece of wood approximately ¾ inch by 2½ inches notched to fit around the transom knee (see Figure 60). Draw a line on each side of the knee.

2. Cut two cleats to fit on each side of the knee, beveled at the top, out of ¾-inch by 1¼-inch stock. Fit them to the lines and fasten them.

3. The next step is to find the shape of the top of the horseshoe seat; we need the top measurement because of the seat bevels back at the transom and on the sides. The bandsaw will only cut these bevels from the top of the plank. Cut lengths of ¾-inch by about 2-inch stock (pine works for this) to fit on the cleats—two to reach across the riser about midway between the thwart location and the transom cleat, and one on the aft side of the thwart location marks. These are the template frames (see Figure 60).

4. The first step in making the template for the after thwart is to cut two strips of wood that measure ¾ inch by 2 inches (pine is fine) to use as cross braces. These will be long enough to reach across the boat on the inside of the fore-and-aft marks that have been made for the after thwart's location.

The ends of the template will be made of two pieces of poster board cut to 8 inches by 4 inches (these will eventually be stapled to the top of the pine cross braces and will act as the top face of the thwart). The thwart will touch the bent frames on either side of the boat. The ends of the thwart are curved and run parallel to the sides of the boat. After fitting the poster board templates to get the right shape, they can then be stapled into place. You are now halfway home. Next, record the bevel on both sides of the template where it intersects the steam-bent frames.

Lay the template onto your 9-inch-wide seat stock and mark the shape of the template ends onto the seat stock. Set your bandsaw to the bevel that you recorded from the frames. You can now cut a little outside the drawn line, and you should have a near-perfect angle on the ends of the thwart. Clean up the cut with your block plane.

The thwart's forward and aft edges are left square.

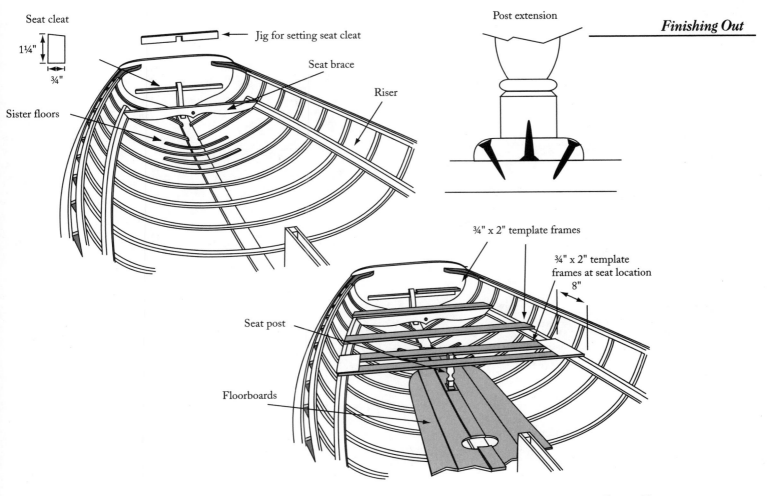

Seat cleat

1¼"

¾"

Jig for setting seat cleat

Seat brace

Riser

Sister floors

Post extension

¾" x 2" template frames

¾" x 2" template
frames at seat location
8"

Seat post

Floorboards

Figure 60:
Install riser and template
Horseshoe seat

5. Now is a good time to fit the turned post under the aft center thwart. (There will be another post under the forward center thwart.) Some people will turn their own posts, but I bought mine at a home improvement store. The space under the seat is somewhere around 10 inches. The store-bought posts can be shortened if too long. If your post is too short, add wood to the top and/or bottom to lengthen it. The posts I bought were 1½ by 1½ inches square. I added a ¾-inch by 2-inch by 2¼-inch piece of Honduras mahogany to the foot, gluing and screwing it through the bottom. The ends are nicely rounded, which makes it easier to screw the post to the floorboard (see Figure 60), centered under the thwart (see Figure 60). The top of the post should extend through the seat template frames. With a straightedge across the bottom of these frames, mark the top of the post. Take the post out, add ¼ inch to these marks, cut the line, and reinstall the post. Then install the thwart over the post. Screw four 1½-inch #8 screws on each side into the risers and one screw through the thwart into the post.

6. Now we will template for the aftermost side seats. Pick one side and measure along the seat brace 6½ inches from the back side of the riser and make a mark. Measure along the aft center thwart 7 inches from the bent frame and make a mark. Fit an 8-inch-wide piece of template stock (⅛-inch tempered Masonite or the equivalent) onto the template frames, within ¼ inch of the transom and bent frames at the sides and onto the thwart (Figure 61). Cover the marks you made on the thwart and seat brace. With a ¾-inch spiling block, mark the intersection of the transom, frames, and thwart. Record the bevels at the bent frames every 1½ inches and the bevel at the transom. Remove the template and place it over the 9-inch seat stock. Mark the outside of the seat shape with the spiling block and cut with the bandsaw to the bevels you took off the sides and the transom. The inside shape will remain a straight edge for now. The end that fits to the thwart remains square.

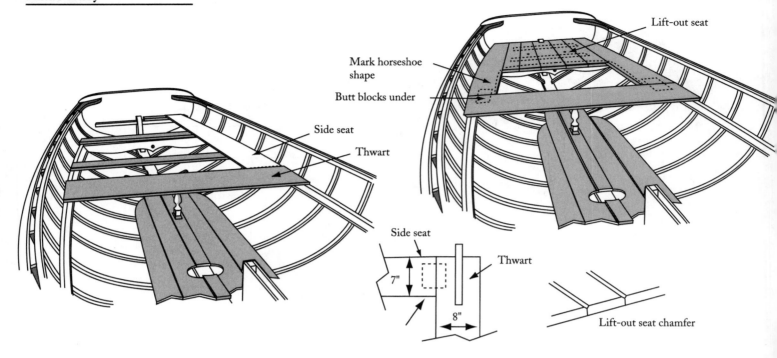

Side seat

Thwart

Side seat

Thwart

7"

8"

Mark horseshoe
shape

Butt blocks under

Lift-out seat

Lift-out seat chamfer

Figure 61:
Install horseshoe seat

7. Fit the side seat into the boat. Do not cut the horseshoe shape yet. Repeat the process on the other side. Screw the side seats to the transom cleats every 2 inches and to the riser every foot. Fit a butt block roughly 5 inches by 5 inches under the seam between the side seats and the thwart, and fasten (see Figure 61).

8. Now make the lift-out seat that fills in the space between the two side seats. Divide the open space between the side seats on the horseshoe seat brace into five equal spaces (see Figure 61). Do the same with the transom seat cleats. Cut and fit pieces of seat stock to fit in the marked spaces. (The center slat will be notched to fit over the knee.) These slats will make up the lift-out part of the seat. It will probably help to use poster board to make a template of this area. Use ¾-inch pine template frames under the poster board to raise the poster board to the height of the top of the seat. Record the bevel at the transom, and fit the template tightly over the transom knee. The aft ends of these slats are beveled to fit to the transom, and the forward end should overlap the forward face of the transom seat brace by 4 to 5 inches. Fit the pieces and then, with your block plane or router, cut a ⅛-inch chamfer on the top side edges (see Figure 61).

9. Fit and screw two ¾-inch by 1½-inch cross braces across the lift-out seat. The forward one should fit snugly behind the seat brace. Drill two ¾-inch holes in the center of the slats on either side of the center slat. Round off the edges of the hole. Use seat stock, Honduras mahogany, or fir for the braces.

10. Using a thin batten, draw the horseshoe shape on the seat. The side seats are approximately 7 inches wide, and the lift-out seat should overlap the front of the seat brace by at least 2 inches. Eyeball this carefully before you cut. symmetry is important! Remove the lift-out seat, cut the line, and round the forward edge with a ⅜-inch radius. Remove the rest of the horseshoe seat and round-over the square edges. Be careful to leave the edges square where the side seats meet the thwart. When it all looks good, fasten everything into the boat, and glue up the butt blocks.

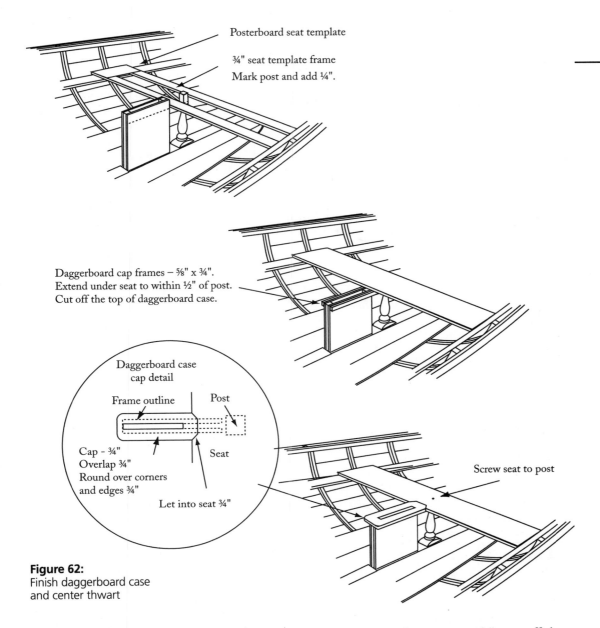

Posterboard seat template

¾" seat template frame
Mark post and add ¼".

Daggerboard cap frames – ⅝" x ¾".
Extend under seat to within ½" of post.
Cut off the top of daggerboard case.

Daggerboard case
cap detail

Frame outline   Post

Cap - ¾"
Overlap ¾"   Seat
Round over corners
and edges ¾"
Let into seat ¾"

Screw seat to post

Figure 62:
Finish daggerboard case
and center thwart

Step H: Fit the forward center thwart and daggerboard case (Figure 62)

1. Template the forward center thwart just as you did the aft center thwart. It butts up against the forward end of the daggerboard case (see Figure 62). Install a post under where the seat will go. Cut out and install the seat. Leave the edges of the seat square.

2. Attach the seat to the centerboard case by making the cap frames. These are made of two pieces of mahogany or fir ⅝ inch (width) by ¾ inch (depth). The cap frames are located along the top of the case and extend under the seat to within ½ inch of the post. Leave the top edges square and round the rest. Screw the cap frames to the ends of the centerboard case and under the seat. Use a square to ensure that the ends line up at the aft end of the daggerboard case. After the frames are fitted, remove the screws, bed, and refasten them.

3. Using the cap frames as a guide, cut off the top of the daggerboard case (see Figure 62) with your handsaw.

4. The daggerboard case cap is ¾ inch by 2⅞ inches by 11 inches. It overlaps the top of the case, the case frames, and the thwart by ¾ inch. The corners of the end that overlaps the thwart are beveled ¾ inch. Mark the overlap onto the thwart. Remove the thwart and cut the seat on the bandsaw. If you cut carefully, leaving the line, you should have little fitting. Cut the slot in the cap the same way you did the daggerboard slot in the keel assembly (Chapter III, Step D, #23; see Figure 26). Round the forward and aft edges of the thwart and the side and aft edges of the cap; then refasten the thwart, and bed and fasten the cap.

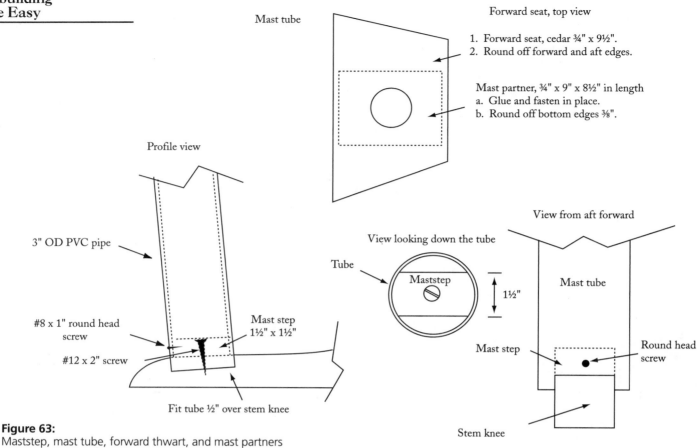

Figure 63:
Maststep, mast tube, forward thwart, and mast partners

Labels within figure:

Mast tube

Forward seat, top view

1. Forward seat, cedar ¾" x 9½".
2. Round off forward and aft edges.

Mast partner, ¾" x 9" x 8½" in length
a. Glue and fasten in place.
b. Round off bottom edges ⅜".

Profile view

3" OD PVC pipe

#8 x 1" round head screw

#12 x 2" screw

Mast step 1½" x 1½"

Fit tube ½" over stem knee

View looking down the tube

Tube

Maststep

1½"

View from aft forward

Mast tube

Mast step

Round head screw

Stem knee

Step I: Fit the forward thwart, mast partners, and maststep (Figure 63)

1. The aft edge of the forward thwart is 34 inches from the forward end of the daggerboard case. It extends forward 9½ inches. Template this thwart the same way as the others. If you don't have stock wide enough, edge-glue narrower pieces with epoxy. Along the center on the bottom of the thwart there is a mast partner ¾ inch by 9 inches by 8½ inches. The grain of the partner runs 90 degrees from that of the seat. The partner is made of seat stock. Glue the partner to the bottom of the seat with epoxy and fasten with 1¼-inch #8 screws. Round the forward and aft edges of the thwart and the bottom edges of the mast partner with a ⅜-inch radius.

2. The mast tube is a length of Schedule 40 PVC pipe about 3 inches outside diameter (OD). This is stock white water pipe. There is also a black pipe, but the wall is thicker. People outside the United States might encounter a different dimension. I wouldn't use an OD much less than 3 inches, as it would make the mast too thin. Sand the outside of the pipe with fine sandpaper to clean off any printing and present a frosted appearance. The pipe should be long enough to go from the hole to the stem with a few inches to spare.

3. Cut a hole in the center of the seat through the partner that allows a slide fit for the tube. Use a hole saw with a hand drill, a circle cutter with a drill press, or a jigsaw. Fasten the thwart to the riser.

4. Fit a piece of wood 1½ inches by 1½ inches by the inside diameter (ID) of the pipe. This is the maststep. Fit the wood into the end of the pipe and push the pipe through the hole until it touches the stem knee. When the pipe is square to the thwart, it should be raking aft. There will be a gap at forward or aft end of the pipe at the stem. Record this gap and use it to cut a bevel on the bottom of the maststep: Mark where the maststep meets the stem knee, then remove the pipe and the maststep, and cut the bevel. Fit the maststep to the stem knee where you marked it, and install it with a 3-inch #12 screw.

5. Cut the bottom of the pipe to the same bevel. Put wedges on each side of the pipe when you cut with the bandsaw. If you don't, it will spin, ruining your blade and probably giving you a nasty bruise or worse.

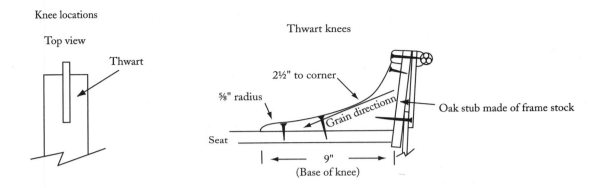

Knee locations

Top view

Thwart

Thwart knees

2½" to corner

⅝" radius

Grain direction

Oak stub made of frame stock

Seat

9"

(Base of knee)

Oarlock pads

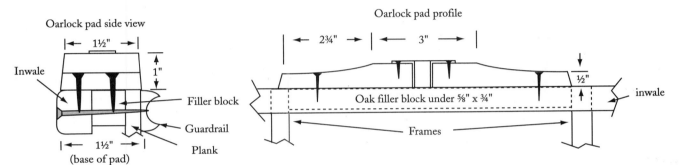

Oarlock pad side view

1½"

Inwale

1"

Filler block

Guardrail

1½"

Plank

(base of pad)

Oarlock pad profile

2¾"

3"

½"

Oak filler block under ⅝" x ¾"

inwale

Frames

Figure 64:
Oarlock pads, thwart knees

6. Fit the pipe through the hole and over the step. Mark where the pipe touches the stem. Use this to cut a notch which allows the pipe to slide tightly over the stem knee ½ inch. When the pipe fits snugly, install a 1-inch #8 round-head screw through the pipe into the after end of the step. Mark around the pipe at the top of the thwart about ¹⁄₁₆ inch above the thwart. Remove the pipe and cut the line. Reinstall the pipe. With a ⅜-inch quarter-round router bit, rout the top of the pipe. This will give you a smooth, rounded, and finished edge at the top of the pipe flush with the seat.

Step J: **Fit the thwart knees** (Figure 64)
Thwart knees are a key structural member in any wooden small craft. They stiffen the structure by creating a girder effect, tying together the thwart, side planks and rails, and, through the posts, the keel. For this boat you will install one knee on each side of the center thwarts and two on each side at the forward thwart (see Figure 58). The knees are installed at 90 degrees to the side of the boat (see Figure 64).

Thwart knees are also an important design detail, and their shape can affect the look of the boat considerably. Heavy, thick-appearing knees run contrary to the flowing lines of a classic Whitehall. Ideally, "grown knees" are used. The builder makes a pattern of the knee and finds a *natural crook* (a fork or curved portion of the trunk, root, or branch) in which the natural flow of the grain follows the curve of the knee. This means that you can drive fastenings through the ends without encountering weak cross-grain, which splits easily. Fruit and nut trees are a good source of grown knees.

If natural crooks are not available, there are a variety of ways to get good structure in a knee. I will show you the one I worked out for my boat. Review Figure 64 carefully.

1. The knees are cut from ¾-inch Honduras mahogany. They will be about ½ inch deep as they fit under the inwale. They are 2½ inches from the center of the curve to the corner at the base and have a ⅝-inch radius at the other end of the base (see Figure 64). The base of the knee is 9 inches long. The center thwart knees are centered on the ends of the thwarts. At the forward thwart the knees are positioned so that the ends of the knees don't extend over the edge of the thwart.

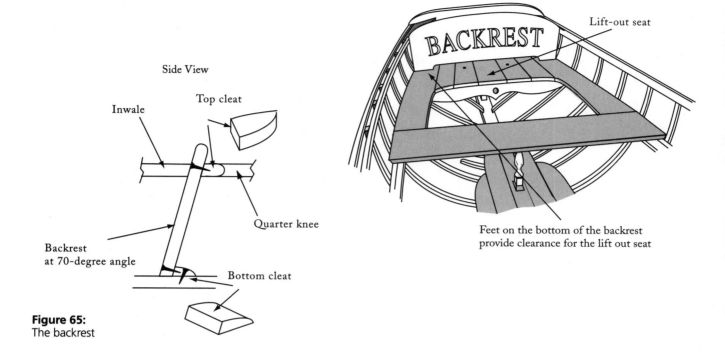

Side View

Inwale

Top cleat

Quarter knee

Backrest
at 70-degree angle

Bottom cleat

Figure 65:
The backrest

Lift-out seat

BACKREST

Feet on the bottom of the backrest
provide clearance for the lift out seat

2. Make a poster board pattern for each knee. There will be a length of ⅝-inch by ¾-inch white oak frame stock installed at each knee location, extending from between the inwale and the sheerstrake over the sheerstrake lap to just under the thwart. This part is fastened through the inwale like the frames were (see Figure 64). The knee is secured by a 2½-inch #8 or #10 screw through the lap and the oak frame piece into the knee. Drive 1¼-inch# 8 screws at the head and the base of the knee.

Step K: Fit the oarlock pads (Figure 64)
Install the oarlock pads as shown in Figure 64. The center of the oarlock socket is 9 inches from the aft end of the thwart. The pads are curved to fit the shape of the rail. There is no need to set the oarlock socket into the pad. Some builders like to do this; others claim it is a water trap. I have done it both ways. Remember to bed the socket, and you should not have a problem.

1. Mark the locations of the oarlock sockets on the rails. The centers of the sockets are 9 inches aft of the after edge of the center seats (see Figure 58). There are four sockets.

2. To make the oarlock pads, make a poster-board template of the footprint of each of the four pads. These are 1½ inches by 8½ inches, curved to fit along the rail. Mark these on 1-inch stock (Honduras mahogany or oak) and cut them out on the bandsaw.

3. Make a template of the profile (see Figure 64), mark it on the pads, and cut them out. Fair the pads with a block plane, spokeshaves, and sand.

4. Out of leftover oak frame stock, make filler blocks between the frames under the oarlock pad locations and fasten through the rails into the filler blocks with 1½-inch #8 screws.

5. Mark the location of the oarlock socket on each pad and drill a hole large enough to accommodate it (a paddle bit will do this job). Locate the pads over the marked locations on the rails, and install the pads with two 1¼-inch #8 screws on each end. Drill through each socket hole through the filler block underneath so that the oarlock shaft can extend through the filler block.

6. Install the oarlock sockets with 1-inch #10 screws. When all fits, remove, bed, and fasten.

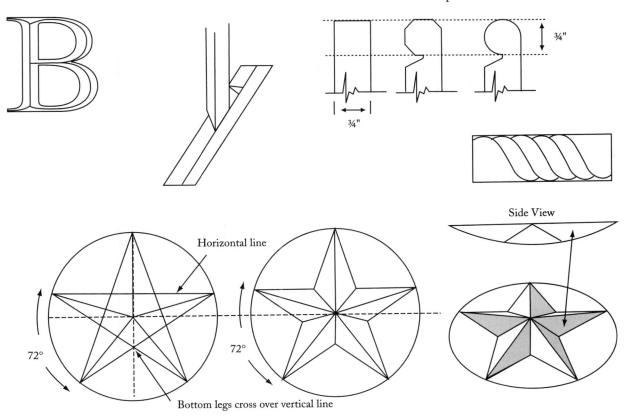

Rope

Side View

Horizontal line

72°   72°

Bottom legs cross over vertical line

Figure 66:
Carving letters and details

Step L: Fit the backrest (Figure 65)

The backrest is optional. However, traditionally the Whitehall boatmen prided themselves on having a well-turned-out backrest. It affords a great chance to display your artistry (see Step M). By now you are an accomplished craftsman, so don't miss the opportunity! The backrest is also the best place to put the name of the boat where you can see it. Remember to make a pattern first. The stock will be ¾-inch by 9½-inch Honduras mahogany.

The backrest is 9½ inches high and crosses the boat at the forward end of the quarter knees. The bottom center is cut away to allow the lift-out seat to clear the backrest. It is a simple installation. The bottom and sides are beveled to fit snugly into the boat. Two cleats at the top and bottom at each side attach the backrest to the boat (see Figure 65). The cleats are glued to the backrest and are not bedded to the boat so that the backrest can be removed for refinishing.

Step M: Carve the boat name and decorative details (Figure 66)

On your backrest pattern you can lay out the lettering and any design elements. In Figure 66 I show you a few classic details, but with a little imagination and reading you can develop a unique and appealing design.

Letters are laid out within lines drawn at the top and bottom of the letters. Roman letters are most popular, but that's up to you. The letters are carved in a V shape (incised), so you need to lay out inside, outside, and center lines throughout the letter. Use a sharp chisel or knife to outline the letter. Then cut straight down at the centerlines and clean out from the sides. A wooden nail file with sandpaper attached works great for smoothing out the cut. If you have not tried marine carving before, I recommend practicing on a piece of pine.

In the drawing I show you how to lay out a star and rope edge as well. These are made by carving away wood around the figures so that they appear raised. For a more detailed description of this work and other ideas, please check out Jay Hanna's *The Shipcarver's Handbook* in Chapter I's bibliography and recommended reading section.

VII
Sailing Rig and Oars

Materials required

Gaff (for lugsail)—spruce or fir, one piece 6/4 by 6/4 rough (1½ inches by 1½ inches finished), 8 feet long.

Sprit (for spritsail)—spruce or fir, one piece 6/4 by 6/4 rough (1½ inches by 1½ inches finished), 13 feet 6 inches long.

Boom—spruce or fir, one piece 6/4 by 6/4 rough (1½ inches by 1½ inches finished), 12 feet long.

Mast—spruce or fir, one piece 5/4 or 6/4 by 5 inches rough, 12 feet long (make two pieces finished four sides 1 inch by 2 inches, 12 feet long).

Oars—spruce or fir, one piece 8/4 by 6 inches rough, 8 feet long.

Traditional rudder—¾-inch mahogany marine plywood (can be glued up from three laminations of 6-millimeter mahogany marine plywood, 2 feet by 3 feet long).

Kick-up rudder—1 sheet 6-millimeter (¼-inch) mahogany marine plywood (enough for daggerboard also); ¼-inch by 1-inch bronze or stainless-steel carriage bolt with wingnut and washer. (Gudgeons and pintles are listed with fittings below.)

Tiller—from oak or Honduras mahogany stock.

Daggerboard—½-inch by 8-inch by 3-foot fir, or two laminations of 6-millimeter (¼-inch) mahogany marine plywood.

Miscellaneous—epoxy, protective gear, solvents, sandpaper, painting and varnishing supplies (see the materials list in Chapter II).

Oar leathers—³⁄₃₂- to ⅛-inch bridle leather, two pieces 8½ by 8 inches, two pieces 1 inch by 18 inches; ½ pint contact cement.

Brass (or bronze) fittings

Two pairs oarlocks.

Gudgeons and pintles—one set each for ¾-inch rudder. Fasten gudgeons with four ¾-inch #10 bronze screws. Fasten pintles with four bronze machine bolts, #8, with nuts and washers: two 2¼-inch for upper pintles, and two 1¼-inch for lower pintles.

Running rigging

Sheet—⅜-inch three-strand nylon rope, 30 feet.

Sail lashing, snotter, traveler—¼-inch three-strand nylon rope, 40 feet; size 4; waxed polyester whipping twine, one roll.

Lashing fairleads—tarred marline, one roll.

Step A: The sail plan (Figures 67, 68)

The traditional rig for Whitehall boats was a spritsail rig with a small jib. This is a handy rig with a reasonable performance that is easy to reduce should the weather turn foul. I chose the standing lug rig (see Figure 67) for this boat, since it has a reputation for better performance. There is a compromise, as the gaff increases weight aloft and somewhat complicates the process of reducing sail in a blow. For those who prefer the sprit rig, I include a sail plan (Figure 68).

Some discussion on how sailboats work is necessary. How well they respond to rudder movements is based on the relationship of the turning moment of the hull, or the center of lateral resistance, and the center of effort of the sail. The center of lateral resistance (CLR) is a point along the waterline that is the midpoint of the area of the underwater profile of the boat. The center of effort (CE) is the center of the area of the sails. There are formulas and endless discussions on what the true relationship of the CLR to the CE is. Generally, the CE leads the CLR by 5 to 10 percent of the waterline length. This can vary considerably from boat type to boat type, and it is recognized that the best way to establish this relationship is to base it on the practical experience of a similar design. To increase *weather helm*, or the ability of the boat to turn, the center of effort is moved farther aft closer to the center of lateral resistance. In a few cases, mostly in catboats, it might actually move aft of the CLR.

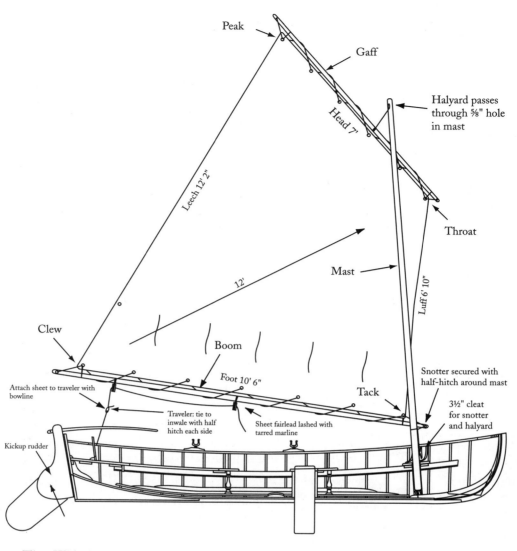

Peak

Gaff

Halyard passes
through ⅝" hole
in mast

Head 7'

Throat

Leech 12' 2"

12'

Mast

Luff 6' 10"

Clew

Boom

Foot 10' 6"

Tack

Snotter secured with
half-hitch around mast

Attach sheet to traveler with
bowline

Traveler: tie to
inwale with half
hitch each side

Sheet fairlead lashed with
tarred marline

3½" cleat
for snotter
and halyard

Kickup rudder

Figure 67:
Standing lug rigging detail

The Whitehall performs surprisingly well, despite its long keel. Modern racing sailboats have a shallow underbody which gets its lateral resistance from a deep, narrow keel balanced with a deep, narrow rudder. Turn the rudder even slightly, and the center of lateral resistance moves forward, which, when coupled with water pressure on the rudder, flings the boat around onto the next tack. Boats with long keels don't work this way. When the rudder is turned, the center of effort barely moves and the water pressure on the rudder tries to overcome the tendency of the long keel to remain on course. Thus the boat has to be "sailed around" to the next tack. This means that sails have to be trimmed with care to maintain boat speed throughout the turn. If the rudder is turned too much, it acts as a brake, and the boat fails to come about. If the rudder is turned too little, the sail luffs as it approaches the direction of the wind, loses speed, and the boat falls off. It takes a little getting used to, but is not a showstopper.

In small boats, one way to shift the CLR forward is to move the weight of the crew forward when coming about or going to weather; this forces the bow under and the stern up. Conversely, when going downwind, shifting the weight aft moves the CLR aft; this increases the underbody profile forward or aft and changes the center of lateral resistance. Sailors of the St. Lawrence Skiff use this technique when they sail their boats without rudders.

Unfortunately, when the weight is shifted forward, the shallow traditional rudder rises up, perhaps totally out of the water, and loses its bite. To remedy this, I have included a design for a kick-up rudder (see Figure 70) that should give better performance. This rudder has sufficient bite to withstand shifts in human ballast and to provide the surface area to help drive the boat through a tack. The kick-up rudder allows you to pull up the blade as you approach shore or strike an underwater object.

The experienced sailor experiments with his or her new boat by shifting weight forward or aft, or by raising or lowering the daggerboard.

(For a more thorough discussion of this subject, see *Classic Small Craft You Can Build* by John Gardner, Mystic Seaport Museum, Mystic, CT, 1993.)

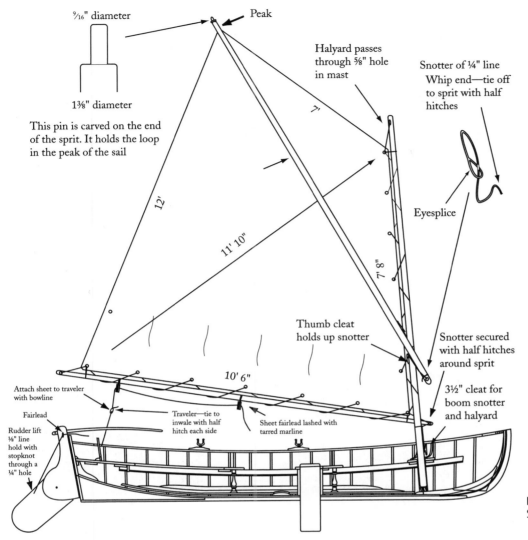

⁹⁄₁₆" diameter

1⅜" diameter

This pin is carved on the end of the sprit. It holds the loop in the peak of the sail

Peak

Halyard passes through ⅝" hole in mast

Snotter of ¼" line
Whip end—tie off to sprit with half hitches

7'

12'

11' 10"

7' 8"

Eyesplice

Thumb cleat holds up snotter

Snotter secured with half hitches around sprit

10' 6"

3½" cleat for boom snotter and halyard

Attach sheet to traveler with bowline

Fairlead

Rudder lift ⅛" line hold with stopknot through a ¼" hole

Traveler—tie to inwale with half hitch each side

Sheet fairlead lashed with tarred marline

Figure 68:
Spritsail rigging detail

Step B: The sail

There are always choices in life. Do I buy a Honda, or do I spring for that BMW? Some of us have no choice, but dream; others opt for the BMW and don't look back. It is the same in the market for traditional sails. Perfectly good sails can be had at a reasonable price. I generally buy this type, because I am always trying to finance my next project and am careful with my budget. Otherwise, I would definitely look at a hand-crafted traditional sail. These sails are awash in extra details that are beautiful to behold and would complement any well-turned-out Whitehall boat. Of course, you will pay dearly for all this fussiness, but many believe the show is worth the entry fee. So, visit many sailmakers and enjoy the experience, and think carefully before you choose.

Step C: Make the daggerboard
(Figure 69)

The daggerboard is a simple device that measures 7½ inches by ½ inch by 3 feet. The cap is two pieces of hardwood ⅝ inch by ¾ inch glued and screwed to the sides at the top (see Figure 69). Round the edges of the cap. You'll also want to round off the edges of the section of the blade that protrudes under the boat; you can easily produce an airfoil shape with your block plane. The blade can be made of vertical-grained fir, or you can laminate together two pieces of 6-millimeter mahogany marine plywood. A length of bungee cord is installed in two holes drilled on each side of the daggerboard cap and secured by stop knots. This bungee cord holds the daggerboard down and can be pulled over the edge of the board so that the board is held in the "up" position. You can put a short length of plastic tubing or a leather sleeve over the bungee cord to prevent it from chafing.

With its long keel, the Whitehall sails just fine off the wind without the daggerboard, so you may want to raise it on some points of sail to reduce drag.

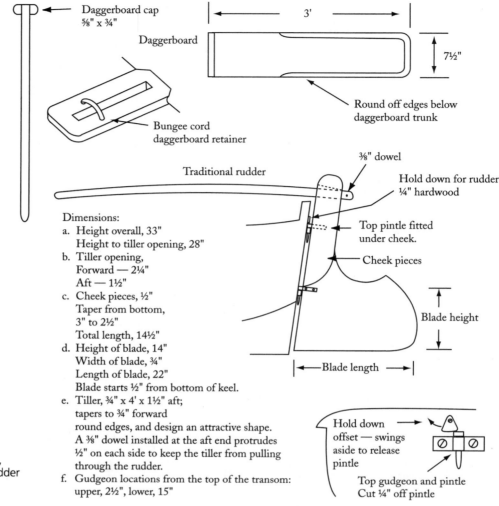

Daggerboard cap
⅝" x ¾"

Daggerboard

3'

7½"

Round off edges below
daggerboard trunk

Bungee cord
daggerboard retainer

⅜" dowel

Traditional rudder

Hold down for rudder
¼" hardwood

Top pintle fitted
under cheek.

Cheek pieces

Blade height

Dimensions:
a. Height overall, 33"
   Height to tiller opening, 28"
b. Tiller opening,
   Forward — 2¼"
   Aft — 1½"
c. Cheek pieces, ½"
   Taper from bottom,
   3" to 2½"
   Total length, 14½"
d. Height of blade, 14"
   Width of blade, ¾"
   Length of blade, 22"
   Blade starts ½" from bottom of keel.
e. Tiller, ¾" x 4' x 1½" aft;
   tapers to ¾" forward
   round edges, and design an attractive shape.
   A ⅜" dowel installed at the aft end protrudes
   ½" on each side to keep the tiller from pulling
   through the rudder.
f. Gudgeon locations from the top of the transom:
   upper, 2½", lower, 15"

Blade length

Figure 69:
Daggerboard,
traditional rudder

Hold down
offset — swings
aside to release
pintle

Top gudgeon and pintle
Cut ¼" off pintle

Step D: Make the rudder (Figures 69–70)
In the past, I built traditional rudders out of solid
lumber (see Figure 69), but I've come to like
building kick-up rudders out of mahogany marine
plywood (see Figure 70). This approach is simpler
in that it does not require gluing up many small
pieces of wood, and works fine. If the ¾-inch (18-
millimeter) plywood cannot be bought in partial
sheets, then by all means buy 6-millimeter and
glue up three layers. Fit the pintles before you
attach the cheeks. There is an opening that ranges
from 2¼ inches to 1½ inches under the cap for the
tiller. The tiller slides through this opening and is
prevented from passing all the way through by the
installation of a ⅜-inch dowel at the aft end. This
tiller is 4 feet long, is adjustable fore-and-aft, and
lifts up to allow the skipper to shift position forward and aft as well as to port and starboard.

The 6-millimeter blade of the kick-up rudder
is drawn up from two 10-inch-diameter circles
whose centers are 15 inches apart. A line is drawn
tangent from the edge of the bottom circle to a
1-inch line extending from the edge of the upper
circle and on the other side a line tangent to both
circles, giving the blade a taper and a ledge to hold
the blade in the "down" position.

For building either type of rudder, steps 1
through 9 are the same.

1. Locate and fasten the gudgeons on the transom; the upper gudgeon is 2½ inches from the top
of the transom, and the lower gudgeon is 15
inches from the top. Draw a centerline, check the
gudgeon locations, and fasten them with four ¾-
inch #10 screws.

2. Draw out all the rudder parts full size on kraft
paper, and cut out the pattern pieces.

3. Lay out the patterns on the plywood stock,
trace, and cut out the parts.

4. Check the fits of the parts, including the pintle locations. The upper pintle will fit under the
cheek pieces. The cheek pieces are mortised out
to fit over the pintle.

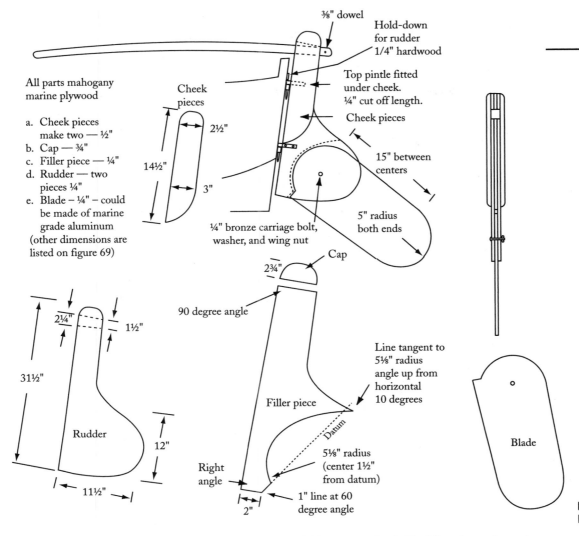

⅜" dowel

Hold-down
for rudder
1/4" hardwood

All parts mahogany
marine plywood

a. Cheek pieces
make two — ½"
b. Cap — ¾"
c. Filler piece — ¼"
d. Rudder — two
pieces ¼"
e. Blade – ¼" – could
be made of marine
grade aluminum
(other dimensions are
listed on figure 69)

Cheek
pieces

2½"

14½"

3"

¼" bronze carriage bolt,
washer, and wing nut

Top pintle fitted
under cheek.
¼" cut off length.

Cheek pieces

15" between
centers

5" radius
both ends

Cap

2¾"

90 degree angle

Filler piece

Line tangent to
5⅛" radius
angle up from
horizontal
10 degrees

Datum

2¼"

1½"

31½"

Rudder

12"

11½"

Right
angle

2"

5⅛" radius
(center 1½"
from datum)

1" line at 60
degree angle

Blade

Figure 70:
Kick up rudder

5. Check the locations of the pintles against the locations of the gudgeons on the transom.

6. Drill holes for two 2¼-inch #8 machine bolts through the cheeks, top pintle, and rudder, and drill for two 1¼-inch bolts for the lower pintles.

7. Dry-fit all the pieces and temporarily fasten to check the fit.

8. If all looks well, disassemble the rudder, glue with epoxy, reinstall the fastenings, clean up the squeezed-out glue, and sand.

9. Cut ¼ inch off the length of the upper pintle, file it round, and smooth the surface. This will allow the lower pintle to enter the lower gudgeon first. If you haven't done this before, trust me—you will love it!

10. For the kick-up rudder, install the pintles, and put a ¼-inch bronze carriage bolt, washer, and wingnut through the rudder and blade.

11. Without a method of holding down the rudder, it will float out of the gudgeons. Make a hold-down as shown out of 6-millimeter plywood or ¼-inch-thick hardwood approximately 1 inch by 1 inch (see Figure 69). It is triangular in shape with a slight radius on the bottom and fastened with a 1-inch #8 round-head wood screw and a washer. Set it off-center so that as the pintle lifts, it will clear the screw.

12. The tiller is made up out of ¾-inch hardwood, preferably oak. It is 4 feet long and is tapered from 1½ inches at the rudder to ¾ inch at the forward end. Round off the edges with your block plane or router with a ¼-inch radius. A little artistry can be added to the tiller by cutting it with a pleasing curve. This should be your design. A ⅜-inch dowel is fitted at the end to keep the tiller from pulling through the rudder. The ends of the dowel protrude ½ inch on each side of the tiller. The dowel can be store-bought or whittled out of hardwood. This arrangement lets you adjust the length of the rudder as you sail by pushing it aft or pulling it forward until it stops on the dowel.

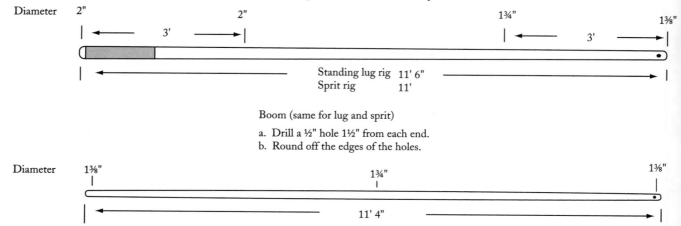

Mast

a. Drill a ⅝" hole for halyard 2" from masthead.
b. Round off the edges of the hole
c. fit and glue ⅛" x 1' 4" leather 2" up from the foot of the mast.

Diameter   2"   2"   1¾"   1⅜"

Standing lug rig   11' 6"
Sprit rig   11'

Boom (same for lug and sprit)

a. Drill a ½" hole 1½" from each end.
b. Round off the edges of the holes.

Diameter   1⅜"   1¾"   1⅜"

11' 4"

Upper end of sprit

⁹⁄₁₆" diameter

1½"

Gaff and sprit

a. Drill a ½" hole 1½" from each end of gaff. 1/2" hole on one end of sprit.
b. Round off the edges of the holes.

Diameter   1⅜"   1¾"   1⅜"

Figure 71:
Spar dimensions

Gaff   7' 8"
Sprit   13'

Step E: Make the spars and fittings
(Figures 71–74)

The spars are all made using the same methods. The rough stock is finished to the widest dimension on the spar. If you have to rough out the stock on the table saw before final planing, leave ¹⁄₁₆ inch on each surface to allow for final planing.

1. Finish and glue up the mast stock: rip the two mast pieces from the rough stock to 1⅛ inches by 2⅛ inches. Plane to a finished dimension of 1 inch by 2 inches and cut off the rough ends to leave a length of 11 feet 6 inches.

2. Glue the pieces up with epoxy, and clamp this assembly to a flat surface (a 2 by 4 or a table) to keep it straight, using pads under the clamps to spread out the clamping pressure. If there is a warp in the stock, reverse the warp in each piece so that by opposing each other, the warps will cancel out. Clean up any epoxy drips immediately. Use clamps on the side to keep the edges of the pieces from slipping over each other. This will give you a mast blank 2 inches by 2 inches by 11 feet 6 inches long.

Follow these steps with all the spars:

3. Size and plane the remaining spar stock (see Figure 71):
Boom—one piece spruce or fir, 1¾ inches square, 11 feet 4 inches long.
Gaff—one piece spruce or fir, 1¾ inches square, 7 feet 8 inches long.
Sprit (substitute for gaff when using the sprit sail plan)—one piece 1¾ inches square, 13 feet long.

4. Draw the mast taper on the mast stock, cut, and plane smooth (Figure 73b).

5. Draw the mast taper on the untapered side, cut, and plane (Figure 73c).

6. Make the eight-siding taper gauge (Figures 72 and 73d) and mark all four sides.

7. Plane the corners off to create eight sides (Figure 73e).

8. Plane to 16 sides.

Finding eight sides from a four-sided figure

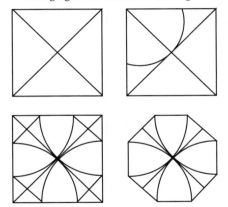

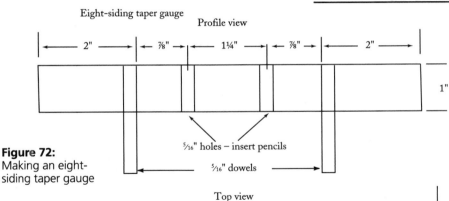

Eight-siding taper gauge

Profile view

2" ⁷⁄₈" 1¼" ⁷⁄₈" 2"

1"

Figure 72:
Making an eight-siding taper gauge

⁵⁄₁₆" holes – insert pencils

⁵⁄₁₆" dowels

Top view

¾"

9. Round the spar. Start by adjusting your block plane to a fine setting. Plane on the ridges, taking long, overlapping strokes. Don't plane over the same area twice, and don't over-plane. When the flats look approximately the same or you seem to be making no progress, stop.

Take a sheet of 100-grit sandpaper and fold it over in thirds. Cup it across the narrow length and push it over the spar in long, overlapping strokes, turning the spar as you go. After a couple of passes, change the process. Now you will grasp the ends of this sheet and, with a shoeshine motion, pull the sandpaper along the spar once again, moving rapidly, overlapping areas, and turning the spar. Resist the temptation to round one small area at a time; bring the whole spar along evenly. You can also cut a 100-grit sanding belt for the shoeshine method.

10. In the boom and the gaff (standing lug rig), drill a ½-inch hole 1½ inches from each end (see Figure 67). Carve a ⁵⁄₁₆-inch-diameter pin 1½ inches long at the top of the sprit; leave square shoulders (see Figures 68 and 71). The sailmaker will sew a rope loop at the peak of the sail that will slide over this pin. Drill a ½-inch hole at the other end.

11. Apply six coats of varnish to the spars (see Chapter VIII).

12. Apply a ⅛-inch by 1-foot-4-inch leather cover to the foot of the mast (see Figure 82) Use bridle leather (from a saddle shop), a well-oiled leather that works well for this purpose. Latigo leather works, too. The leather should wrap around the mast with a ½-inch overlap. With a sharp chisel or knife, trim a ½-inch bevel (scarf) on the ends of the leather so that the top overlap will feather into bottom overlap. Then coat the underside of the leather and the rough cut of the bevel with contact cement. Where the leather will lie, coat the mast with contact cement right over the varnish. When the cement skins over, wrap the leather over the mast, lining up the scarfs, and wrap the finished leather with a bicycle inner tube cut open to clamp it in place. Let it set overnight.

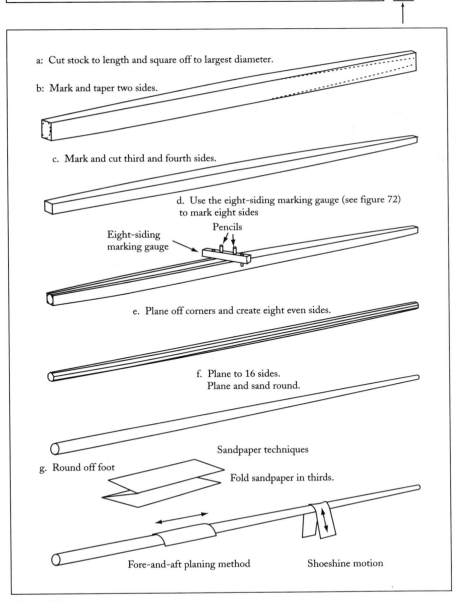

a: Cut stock to length and square off to largest diameter.

b: Mark and taper two sides.

c. Mark and cut third and fourth sides.

d. Use the eight-siding marking gauge (see figure 72) to mark eight sides

Eight-siding marking gauge

Pencils

e. Plane off corners and create eight even sides.

f. Plane to 16 sides.
Plane and sand round.

g. Round off foot

Sandpaper techniques

Fold sandpaper in thirds.

Fore-and-aft planing method

Shoeshine motion

Figure 73:
Shaping the mast

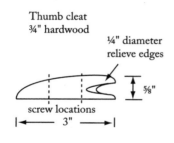

Thumb cleat
¾" hardwood

¼" diameter
relieve edges

⅝"

screw locations

|← 3" →|

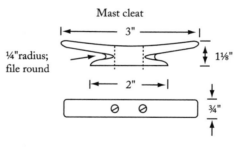

Mast cleat

|← 3" →|

¼"radius;
file round

1⅛"

|← 2" →|

¾"

Sheet fairlead

1½"

Radius ¼"

Figure 74:
Fittings for sailing rig

Note: All fittings are made of hardwoods.

13. In rigging these small boats, it is easy to make your own spar fittings. Figure 74 shows several fittings that you can make for your boat. They are roughed out on the bandsaw and finished out with a sharp knife, chisel, files, and sandpaper. A medium rattailed file and a half-round file should do the trick. Sandpaper wrapped around a pencil works well also. Change grits, and you can rough out and finish in short order.

a. With size 4 waxed polyester waxed whipping line, make a loop

b. Wrap whipping around the line holding the loop to the line. Leave tail showing.

Tail

c. Continue wrap until within ¼" of the end of the line.

d. Pass the end of the whipping through the loop.

e. Holding on to the end, pull the tail until the end is pulled under the whipping.

f. Cut off the exposed end and tail

Figure 75:
Whipping the end of a line

Step F: Rig the boat
(Figures 67–68, 74–76)
As you sail this boat, you will develop your own rigging details. Most people do. Here is a good place to start.

1. For the standing lug rig, lash the sail to the boom and gaff (see Figure 67) by looping ¼-inch three-strand nylon line twice through the hole at the end of the spar and the grommet at the sail tack or throat. Lace the line around the spar, and repeat the loops at the other end. Adjust the sail along the spar until the sail is even; then pull the ends tight and secure with two half-hitches (see Figure 76). Cut the line to length, leaving 3 feet of line attached to the forward end of the boom for the snotter. Whip the ends of the line (see Figure 75). For the sprit rig (see Figure 68), lash the foot of the sail on the boom and rig the same as for the lug rig.

2. To cut the line, I have an attachment for my soldering gun that uses a hot copper blade to cut the line. It cuts and burns the ends at the same time. You can do the same thing with a hot knife, or use a cold knife and burn the end with a match or cigarette lighter.

3. For the lug rig, about a third of the way up the gaff, tie the halyard with a clove hitch followed by two half-hitches around the halyard. Pass the end of the halyard through the hole at the top of the mast. Set the mast in the mast tube and raise the sail. Temporarily tie off the halyard over the inwale.

4. For either rig, wrap the boom snotter around the mast and pull the end of the boom into the mast. Pass a half-hitch over the snotter and tie off with a timber hitch on the mast to hold it temporarily.

5. Make or buy a 3-inch mast cleat (see Figure 74). Locate it on the mast about 6 inches below the location of the boom when the sail is raised. Tie the halyard to this and tie the boom snotter over it.

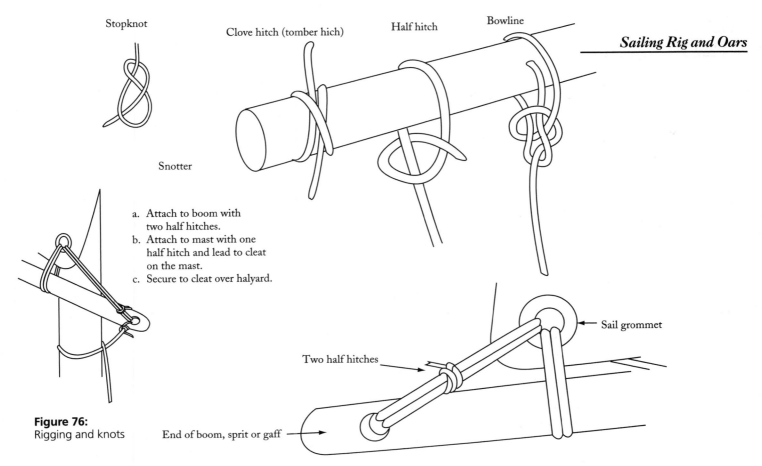

Stopknot

Clove hitch (tomber hich)

Half hitch

Bowline

Snotter

a. Attach to boom with two half hitches.
b. Attach to mast with one half hitch and lead to cleat on the mast.
c. Secure to cleat over halyard.

Sail grommet

Two half hitches

Figure 76:
Rigging and knots   End of boom, sprit or gaff —▶

6. For the sprit rig lash the luff of the sail as shown in Figure 81. Run the line around the mast, through the grommet and then instead of continuing around the mast, reverse direction around the mast. This is a traditional way of lashing to the mast that insures that the lashing loosens evenly when you release the halyard. Continuing around in a continuous loop as you did with the boom leads to the lashing hanging up when released.

7. To raise the peak of the sprit sail, place the pin at the top of the sprit into the rope eye at the peak of the sail and push the sprit up until the sail sets about right (see Figure 68). Wrap the snotter (a 3-foot length of ¼-inch line with an eyesplice at one end) around the mast and back through the eye. Then run the end of the snotter through the ½-inch hole at the end of the sprit and set the sprit. Tie off the snotter with two half-hitches around the sprit just above the hole (see Figure 76). When you have located where the snotter sets best, screw the thumb cleat to the mast to hold up the eyesplice (see Figure 68).

8. The traveler (see Figures 67 and 68) is a piece of ¼-inch line about 3 feet 6 inches long. Secure it at the inwales with two half-hitches at each side of the boat, just forward of the backrest. Do not cut off the ends of the line until you have used the traveler several times, to get the right length.

9. Make two sheet fairleads (see Figure 74). Starting with a timber hitch, wrap six or seven loops of tarred marline around the boom and the fairlead, leaving a ½-inch gap between the boom and the fairlead. Wrap the marline around the loops at this gap, pulling all tight. Tie off with half-hitches. Place one fairlead 1 foot after the end of the boom and one 3 feet aft. After you have sailed the boat for a while, these can be easily moved.

10. Whip the ends of all lines (Figure 75).

11. The painter is a ⅜-inch line used to temporarily tie the boat up. It is passed through ⅝-inch holes drilled at the bow on each side in the plank just below the sheerstrake (see Figure 84). The holes are drilled 1½ inches from the rabbet and centered in the plank. Use a paddle bit or a Forstner bit to drill the hole, and hold a ¾-inch wood block behind where the drill will come through the plank so that the drill won't damage the exit hole. Round the hard edges of the hole about ⅟₁₆ inch with 150-grit sandpaper, and seal them with epoxy glue.

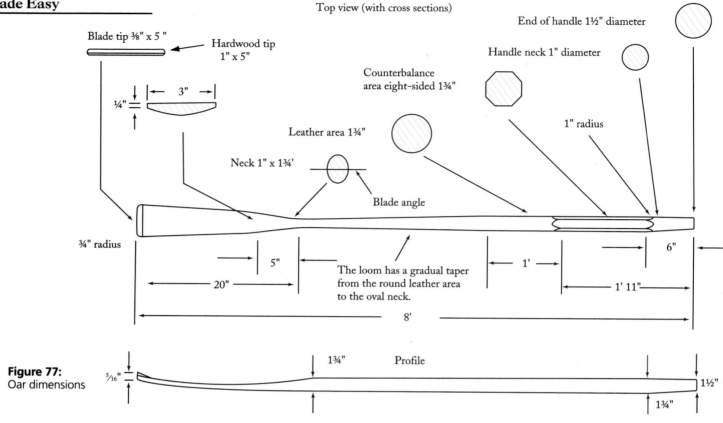

Top view (with cross sections)

End of handle 1½" diameter

Blade tip ⅜" x 5"

Hardwood tip
1" x 5"

Handle neck 1" diameter

Counterbalance
area eight-sided 1¾"

¼"   3"

Leather area 1¾"

1" radius

Neck 1" x 1¾'

Blade angle

¾" radius

5"

The loom has a gradual taper
from the round leather area
to the oval neck.

1'

6"

20"

1' 11"

8'

Figure 77:
Oar dimensions

⁵⁄₁₆"

1¾"   Profile

1½"

1¾"

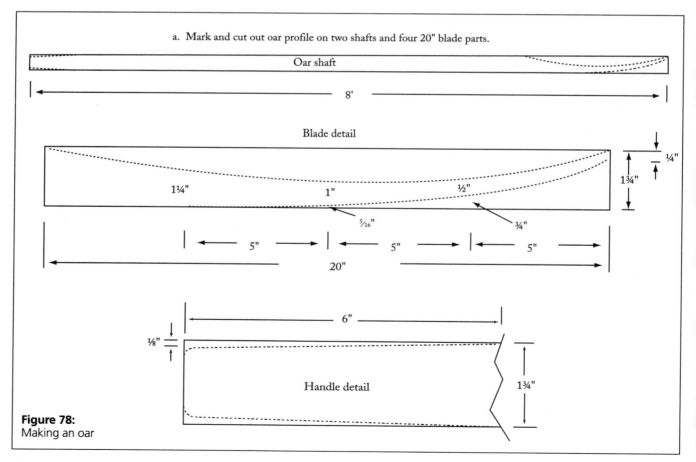

a. Mark and cut out oar profile on two shafts and four 20" blade parts.

Oar shaft

8'

Blade detail

¼"

1¾"

1¼"   1"   ½"

⁵⁄₁₆"   ¾"

5"   5"   5"

20"

6"

⅛"

Handle detail

1¾"

Figure 78:
Making an oar

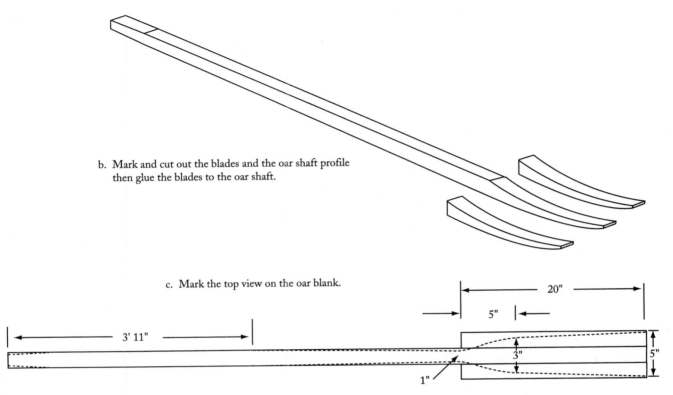

b. Mark and cut out the blades and the oar shaft profile then glue the blades to the oar shaft.

c. Mark the top view on the oar blank.

Figure 79:
Making an oar (continued)

d. Cut out the top view.

Step G: Make the oars (Figures 77–82)
Milling the oar stock— spruce or fir, 8/4 by 6-inch by 8 feet long, rough
Rip the oar stock into three pieces, 1⅞ inches square. Mill these pieces to 1¾ square.
Cut one of the three pieces into 2-foot lengths.

Next, line out the oars:

1. Mark and cut out the oar profile on the two shafts (this includes the blade and the handle). Mark and cut out the blade profile on the four 2-foot blade pieces. Glue the blade pieces to the shaft as shown (Figure 79b).

2. Mark the top view on the oar stock and cut it out (Figure 79c and 79d).

3. Fair the curve of the blade with your spoke-shave and sand smooth. A sanding block shaped to the curve of the deepest part of the blade will help in fairing this part of the blade (see blade detail in Figure 78).

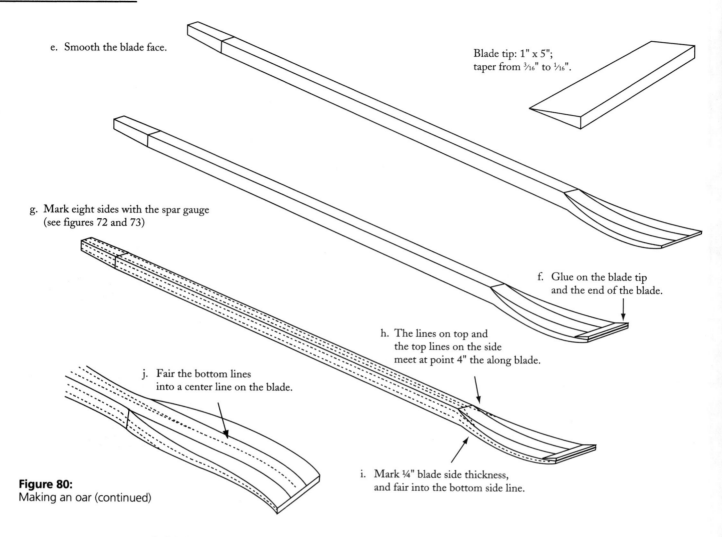

e. Smooth the blade face.

Blade tip: 1" x 5";
taper from ³⁄₁₆" to ¹⁄₁₆".

g. Mark eight sides with the spar gauge
(see figures 72 and 73)

f. Glue on the blade tip
and the end of the blade.

h. The lines on top and
the top lines on the side
meet at point 4" the along blade.

j. Fair the bottom lines
into a center line on the blade.

i. Mark ¼" blade side thickness,
and fair into the bottom side line.

Figure 80:
Making an oar (continued)

4. Make two wedges of hardwood ³⁄₁₆ inch by 1 inch by 5 inches and glue them onto the tip of the blades as shown in Figure 80.

5. To shape the looms of the oars, you'll follow roughly the same steps as for shaping the spars (Step E, #1-7, Figures 72 and 73). First, mark on the oar stock the shaping guidelines for eight-siding the oar shaft from the handle to the blade (Figure 80g). You can use the spar gauge here.`

6. On top of the blade, continue the two lines on the shaft to points 4 inches along each side of the blade, making continuous and fair lines (Figure 80h).

7. On the bottom of the blade, continue the two lines on the shaft to a centerline drawn on the blade. These lines should merge with the centerline with a fair and gradual taper (Figure 80i).

8. To line out the side of the blade, mark a line ¼ inch down on each side at the tip. Continue the line parallel to the top. At two-thirds of the way back from the tip, let this line gradually leave the top until it fairs into the bottom eight-side marking line on the side of the shaft. The top line on the side fairs from the shaft to the point located 4 inches along the blade where it meets the line on the top of the blade (Figure 80j).

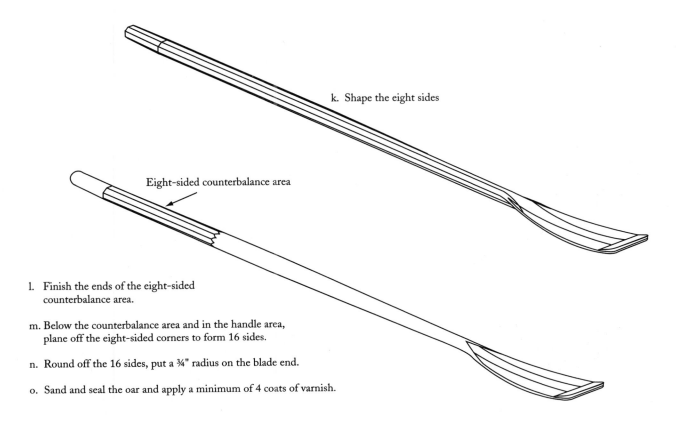

k. Shape the eight sides

Eight-sided counterbalance area

l. Finish the ends of the eight-sided counterbalance area.

m. Below the counterbalance area and in the handle area, plane off the eight-sided corners to form 16 sides.

n. Round off the 16 sides, put a ¾" radius on the blade end.

o. Sand and seal the oar and apply a minimum of 4 coats of varnish.

Figure 81:
Making an oar (continued)

9. With your spokeshave and block plane, shape the eight sides of the oar shaft. Be careful to keep the facets the same on both oars.

The cross-grain at the deepest point in the valley of the blade face can be difficult to fair with hand tools. Careful use of a belt sander will clean up the blade area; or use a curved sanding block with 80- to 60-grit sandpaper mounted on the block with contact cement. Fair the hardwood tip in with the rest of the blade. A one-third-sheet finishing sander with 60- to 80-grit sandpaper can help in rounding the bottom of the blade.

10. Mark the handle around the stock at 6 inches and the end of the eight-sided area at 1 foot 11 inches (see Figure 77). Round the handle and shaft as you did the spars, leaving the eight-sided counterbalance area to give a contrast. The back of the blade you can shape to suit your eye.

11. Finish off with a folded sheet of sandpaper. Sand with 100-grit and then 150-grit, being careful to sand with the grain. Apply a minimum of four coats of varnish; six coats is best (see Chapter VIII for tips on varnishing).

12. After the varnish is set, apply the leathers (Figure 82). The leather goes on the same as the mast leather (Step E, #10), except that a button is added. The button is a 1-inch-wide strip of leather that makes two wraps around the oar leather and is beveled on each end about ¾ inch so that it lies flat. Apply these leathers with contact cement. Clamp in place with bungee cord or wrap with a bicycle innner tube.

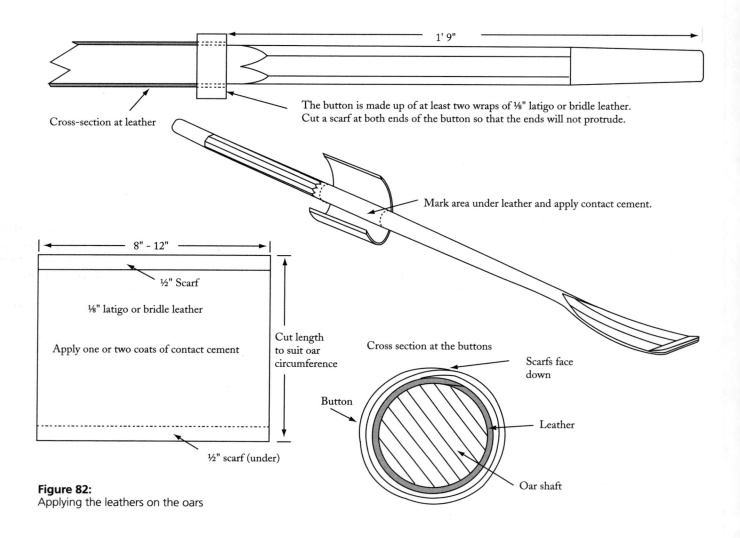

1' 9"

Cross-section at leather

The button is made up of at least two wraps of ⅛" latigo or bridle leather. Cut a scarf at both ends of the button so that the ends will not protrude.

Mark area under leather and apply contact cement.

8" - 12"

½" Scarf

⅛" latigo or bridle leather

Apply one or two coats of contact cement

Cut length to suit oar circumference

½" scarf (under)

Cross section at the buttons

Scarfs face down

Button

Leather

Oar shaft

Figure 82:
Applying the leathers on the oars

VIII
Finishing Touches

Materials required

Marine enamel or high-quality oil-based enamel—1 quart primer; 3 quarts finish paint (1 quart each for the outside, the inside, and for contrasting floorboards and seats).

Paint additive (brushing liquid)—1 quart penetrol or boiled linseed oil (to make paint flow and reduce brush drag without excessive thinning).

Spar varnish, with ultraviolet filter—1 pint, for spars, transom, and rails (varnish more if you can't resist, but remember that this increases maintenance; it sure does look good, though!).

Thinners—1 gallon paint thinner (for thinning paint and brush cleanup); 1 quart lacquer thinner (for polyurethane bedding cleanup; stove alcohol, also known as denatured alcohol, works too).

Fillers—exterior wood filler for screw holes; painter's surfacing putty for minor dents and dings.

Enamel sign paint—¼ pint, for bead and/or lettering.

Painting/varnishing supplies

Sandpaper—aluminum oxide, 80-, 100-, 150-grit, 220-grit wet-or-dry.

Masking tape—light-release, one roll.

Paintbrushes—china bristle, minimum of 2-inch, 1½-inch, and 1-inch widths.

Rags, paper towels—for cleanup.

Protective gear—Latex gloves; respirator with filters suitable for solvent fumes.

Rope fender (if desired)—⅝-inch three-strand nylon rope, 20 feet; size 16 waxed polyester whipping twine, one roll; ⅝-inch #6 stainless-steel pan-head self-tapping screws, 18.

Bow line (painter)—⅜-inch three-strand nylon rope, 10 feet.

Brass (or bronze) fittings

Eyebolt for trailer—brass (or bronze), 1-4-inch by 4 inches, with nut and washer.

Stem band—⅝-inch brass half-oval, 3 feet long.

Keel shoe—3/32-inch or ⅛-inch by 1-inch brass strap, 12 feet long.

Bronze screws—¾-inch #8 flat-head, 25.

Step A: Varnish

By now you have probably decided what you will paint and what you will varnish. By all means, varnish the oars and spars. Let me counsel you once again that the amount of maintenance you'll have will be in direct relationship to how much of the boat you finish bright (varnish). This is particularly true if the boat is stored in the sunshine for long periods. Varnish deteriorates in sunlight. Using a high-quality marine varnish with an ultraviolet shield is a must, but even this will deteriorate in a season of sunshine. The easiest way to keep varnish bright is to protect it from the sun with covers or by storing the boat in a shed.

In my early years in California I had a small sailboat with varnished decks which I sailed every day and tied to a dock in direct sunlight 12 months of the year. I noticed that for about a month after I applied varnish, water would bead on the finish. For about another two months, the varnish would look fine, but at the end of this period, the shine would be fading. If I didn't put on another coat in six months, the varnish might start flaking, and some wood, like oak, might start showing black marks. To keep up the finish, I would start out the year with a thorough sanding to clean off deteriorated layers. Then I would put on two coats of varnish, allowing two to three weeks between coats for the varnish to cure; this would allow for each coat to harden before I put on the next. I would apply a third coat in late July just before the hottest days of summer and another in September just after the hottest days. That would usually keep the boat looking ship-shape through the season. If the varnish is kept up, there should be no need to strip for many years. Whatever your climate and latitude, the way to keep varnish up is to have a maintenance schedule and stick to it.

Plan on putting at least six coats of varnish on your new boat as soon as is practical. You should plan to lay down at least four coats before launching and another two soon after, sanding between all coats. I like to varnish before I paint; otherwise, I run the risk of paint soaking into the grain of the wood where I want to varnish, which requires a finicky cleanup. I start by sanding carefully along the grain with 100- and 150-grit sandpaper on the areas I want to varnish. Then I wipe down these areas with paint thinner on a rag. This cleans up the dust while exposing cross-grain scratches, which will show up as black lines. Sand or plane out these areas and sand again. When all looks fine, sand carefully with 220-grit paper. Then mask off the paint areas.

Use only fresh varnish, and never shake or stir it. Pour off the varnish you want to use into a clean can and cover the varnish can immediately. With an awl, poke holes every 2 inches in the groove at the top of the can; this will allow any varnish caught in the top of the can to drip back into the can. Buy only as much varnish as you plan to use. Varnish can gel in the can over time and may, in the long run, lose its drying ability.

Before you start, read the can carefully. Get a thinner that is compatible with your varnish. Usually thinning 10 percent is recommended. Thinning is a good practice all the time, and, for the first coat, allows the varnish to penetrate and act as a sealer. Thin coats will lay down and cure faster. I like to brush on a well-thinned sealer coat followed by a thorough sanding, then apply the second coat. Brush with the grain. Feather out the edges of the varnish before you get more varnish, and skip along to start your next strokes, feathering back into the last area. Work quickly but thoroughly. Once the varnish is brushed down, finish up with long strokes toward the new area. After two coats, I move on to priming the paint areas; then back to another varnish coat, a finish coat of paint, another coat of varnish, then a finish coat of paint. This gives the paint and varnish coats time to cure.

The first coats of varnish require more sanding than later coats, as you will be fairing the surface for two to four coats, depending on the depth of the grain. If the wood has a deep grain, you will have sanded a lot of the varnish off in the fairing process, so this is why you need at least six coats to get good protection. Be sure to use a quick-release masking tape, as many tapes have adhesives that will eat up fresh paint and pull the paint off when the masking tape is removed. It is also good practice to pull off the tape within an hour after you have finished a coat. This will save you real problems. As it is, paint needs at least a month to harden up, and care should be taken to protect the painted surfaces from hard knocks before that.

Wear latex or rubber gloves when varnishing, painting, and cleaning brushes. In close quarters, wear a respirator with a filter designed for solvent and paint fumes. It is not unusual for people to develop sensitivities to solvents, and prolonged inhalation of the fumes can be dangerous, so work smart and protect yourself. Pour used thinner into a empty thinner can and reuse it for the early stages of brush cleaning. Dispose of all solvents at a hazardous-waste center.

Keep your work area as dust free as possible. A shop vacuum is better than stirring the dust with a broom. Wetting the floor also helps keep dust down.

Step B: Paint

Paint is another story. I have used marine paints and high-quality oil-based house paint on small wooden boats, and both work. The paints sold for marine use are usually faster-drying than house paints, have lower viscosity, cure harder, and are designed to be applied on carefully prepped primer. The house paints are thick with solids, tend to harden more slowly, and are designed to be "one-coat" finishes. The house paints have the advantage of a greater variety of colors. After exposure to sunlight they tend to lose their gloss and leave a flat finish, which is not necessarily bad for a traditional boat.

Lately I have been using marine finishes purchased at one of those hardware super stores. The paint is half the price of the paints bought at marine stores, and you can ask the store to create colors for you. They can tint the primer, too. This will make it easier for the finish coats to cover the primer. Save the formulas so that you can match the colors again. I was able to get both high-gloss and satin finishes at the super store. For the inside of the boat, I like to use a satin finish, as it is hard to sand these areas and difficult to ensure that all surfaces are adequately roughed up in preparation for the next coat. If satin finishes are not available, add 10 to 15 percent primer to the finish paint. This will flatten it and also add solids for better coverage. For lettering or painting a bead along the sheerstrake (see Chapter IV, Step F, #34), I use sign painter's enamel, a one-coat enamel that is great for those areas where multiple coats are difficult. Remember, when you open the paint can, to take an awl and poke holes every 2 inches around the rim of the can to allow the paint to drain out of the can's lip.

Use only high-quality china bristle brushes. There are good brushes that are reasonably priced, so you don't have to spend a fortune. For this boat, you should have a 1½-inch and a 2-inch brush at least, and a ¼-inch medium stiff artist's brush for any beading or lettering.

I use two types of fillers. One is a standard hardware-store-variety exterior wood filler for filling screw holes, and the other is a surfacing putty from the marine store to fix up shallow surface imperfections. Both are white or light-colored to make it easy for the finish coats to cover. Before I start to paint, I fill the screw holes with the wood filler. I use the surfacing putty after the first primer coat. Different manufacturers have different names for their products, so the best way to avoid confusion is to go to the store and read the cans carefully.

The secret of any good finish is in the prep work. Most deep brushstrokes that show in the final finish come through from the primer coats. To avoid this, the first primer coat should be thinned 15 percent. Do not thin in the paint can. Pour some paint into a clean container and cover the can. This first coat is a wash coat to soak into the wood and become the foundation of your finish. Many paints have a noticeable brush drag right out of the can which only disappears after you thin them substantially. Unfortunately, overly thinned paint can be translucent and lose its ability to cover. To prevent overthinning, painters use additives containing boiled linseed oil, such as penetrol; this allows the paint to flow without excessive thinning.

Sand the wash coat carefully; just scrub the first coat lightly with 150-grit to knock down any roughness. Next lay on a thicker coat of primer. Thin it slightly with thinner and add penetrol until the paint flows. This coat will require more sanding to get rid of brush marks. (Fill again if you have to.) Be careful not to sand through the primer, especially on hard corners. Touch up any areas that you sand through with thinned primer. Beginners often end up with three coats of primer.

Paint colors are a matter of preference. You should keep in mind that light colors stay cool in sunlight and prevent the boat from drying out excessively. Traditional hull colors would be white or off-white. Dark colors are to be avoided, although you may get away with painting the sheerstrake dark if the boat doesn't spend its days in direct sunlight.

Before you apply paint, fill the end of the brush with paint, lift it up, and allow the paint to drip back into the container. Observe the way the paint drips. It is best when it is an even stream—neither runny nor thick. As you brush, you will feel when the paint is laying on the best. You want to brush on the most paint you can without drag, and only enough so that you can lay it down in a nice, even coat. When you are happy with the feel, do the drip test again; this will give you a sign when your thinning process is just right. You will have to add more thinner as you go to allow for evaporation; expect to add more on a hot day. Do not over-thin, use too small a brush, or over-brush. Clean your brushes thoroughly, and wrap them with paper towels and store them flat or hang them. Pour your used thinner into an empty thinner can. Keep it separate from your used varnish thinner, as the paint will settle out of the thinner if it is allowed to sit for a while. Most of the solids will drop out of the thinner within a week or two.

The "wet edge" of the paint, or the period when the paint will lay down without leaving brush marks, is only a few minutes. Brush the paint on with the grain, then make quick strokes across the grain, then brush with the grain again. Feather the edges of the paint area you are working. When you load the brush again, lightly scrape the excess paint off into the paint container. Skip a foot along the painting surface, and feather the paint back into the previously painted area. When this is joined, brush forward, leaving a feather edge at the end.

Painting and varnishing are skills that improve with practice. Take your time with preparation, be aware of what is happening at the end of your brush, and keep track of the feel and drip of the paint. Good luck!

It is helpful to check your finish as you go to pick up missed or flat areas. A bright light will help. Once the paint is tacky, don't try to brush these areas; the brush will drag and ruin the finish. If you find a drip, roll over a piece of masking tape and touch the sticky side to the drip. The paint will fair out if you find the drip soon enough, and if not, at least you won't have a drip of jellied paint in the middle of your paint job.

Step C: Install the rope fender
(Figure 83)
Now you can add the last finishing touches and launch your boat. The rope fender for the cove in the guardrail (see Chapter IV, Step B, Figure 56) is made of a 20-foot length of ⅝-inch nylon three-strand rope, available in either black or white (those who will be running against tarred pilings might consider black). Start by burning the ends of the line. Then whip one end with heavy whipping twine (size 16). Place the whipped end of the line into the groove in the guardrail at the transom, and mark where the forward end of the whipping strikes the rail. Drill a ¹⁄₁₆-inch pilot hole ¼ inch deep in the rail here and every 1½ feet, up to and including 2 inches before the stem. Drive a ⅝-inch #6 stainless-steel self-tapping pan-head screw between the upper strands of the rope and through the lowest strand into the pilot hole. The screw will disappear under the top two strands and be invisible (see Figure 83). Stretch the rope to the next pilot hole. Drive a screw through the rope just aft of the pilot so that the screw pulls the rope up to the hole. Continue down the rail. Drill a pilot on the other side of the boat 2 inches from the stem and every 1½ feet until you are near the stern. Pull the rope tight and install the screws. At the stern, pull the stretch out of the rope and determine how much line is needed to reach the transom, whip the end, trim the excess line, and burn the cut end. Drill a pilot hole just forward of the whipping and install a screw through the rope.

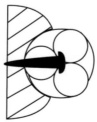

Figure 83:
The rope fender

Step D: Install the painter, stem band, shoe, and eyebolt (Figure 84)

1. The painter is a length of ⅜-inch three-strand nylon line. I have specified 10 feet, but it could be longer. It is used for tying the boat up for short periods of time. It is passed through the ⅝-inch holes in the planks at the bow and tied to itself with a bowline or an eyesplice. Any good knot book will describe how to make an eyesplice, which is handy knowledge to have.

2. Install the 4-inch by ¼-inch eyebolt for the trailer through the stem about 10 inches down. Then, from a 3-foot length of ⅝-inch brass half-oval, cut a length to fit the stem face over the eyebolt. Round the ends, grind a decorative detail at the top end (see Figure 84), and drill and countersink at each end for a ¾-inch #8 bronze screw. As shown in Figure 84, you can add a decorative touch to the stem band. I use a bench grinder for this, but files will work as well. Remove the scratches with sandpaper, going from rough to fine, and polish it with brass polish. Round the ends of the remaining half-oval. Drill holes and countersinks in the ends of the half-oval for #8 screws, drill and countersink at approximately 8-inch intervals, and install the stem band below the eyebolt. You can buy countersinks that work in metal from the hardware store. Bring one of your screws with you, and make sure that the angle of the countersink matches your screw.

3. The shoe is a length of 1-inch by ³⁄₃₂-inch or ⅛-inch brass strap which extends from the end of the half-oval to the forward end of the dagger-board slot and continues from the after end of the slot, bending over the end of the keel and 3 inches up the sternpost. This protects the keel from rough landings. To fasten it, drill and countersink for #8 screws at the ends and every 8 inches. Grind a decorative design on the end of the strap (see Figure 84).

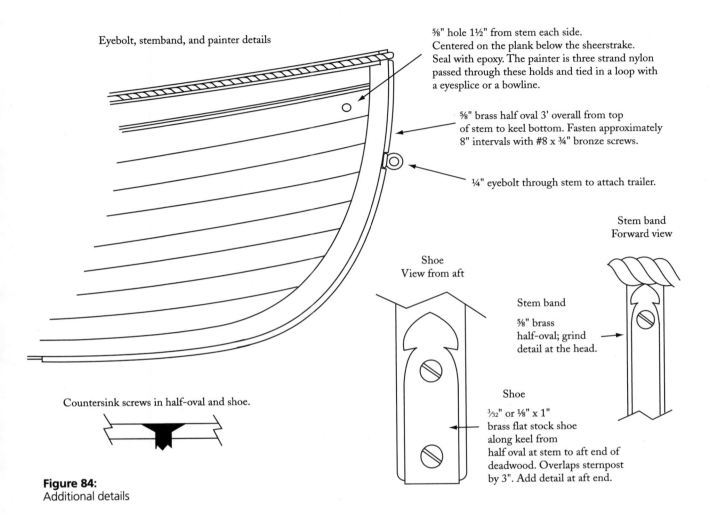

Eyebolt, stemband, and painter details

⅝" hole 1½" from stem each side. Centered on the plank below the sheerstrake. Seal with epoxy. The painter is three strand nylon passed through these holds and tied in a loop with a eyesplice or a bowline.

⅝" brass half oval 3' overall from top of stem to keel bottom. Fasten approximately 8" intervals with #8 x ¾" bronze screws.

¼" eyebolt through stem to attach trailer.

Shoe View from aft

Stem band Forward view

Stem band ⅝" brass half-oval; grind detail at the head.

Shoe ³⁄₃₂" or ⅛" x 1" brass flat stock shoe along keel from half oval at stem to aft end of deadwood. Overlaps sternpost by 3". Add detail at aft end.

Countersink screws in half-oval and shoe.

Figure 84:
Additional details

Step E: Fit the boat to the trailer

Fit the boat to the trailer carefully. Support the keel with at least three rollers, letting the full weight of the boat rest on the rollers. (Do not support the weight of the boat on the hull planking.) Have adjustable supports holding the boat upright. For my boat, I adapted fittings that came with the trailer. Do not use a winch to pull the boat onto the trailer; this will put unnecessary stress on the boat and could damage it. Float it or lift it on the trailer and use the winch to guide it.

Step F: Protect your leathers

Keep your mast and oar leathers well oiled with a good-quality oil. If you do a lot of rowing, you will have to lubricate the oar leathers. The old-timers used tallow which they made themselves, but there are a variety of goos that will do. A friend mixes Vaseline and paraffin.

To make tallow, old-timers cut the fat scraps from their dinner and heated it at a heat that minimizes smoking. They poured off the grease, which came out somewhat dark, then added water and simmered it for quite a while until the dark stuff settled out. Then this mess was cooled and the hard tallow taken out. My old friend R. D. "Pete" Culler was the master of such recipes and delved into these mysteries in his books, including *Skiffs and Schooners* and *Boats, Oars and Rowing*. If you can find his books somewhere, buy them.

You haven't launched yet? Better get going, and have fun!